NUTRITION & HEALTH

Diet and Disease

BONNIE JUETTNER

LUCENT BOOKS
A part of Gale, Cengage Learning

GALE
CENGAGE Learning™

Detroit • New York • San Francisco • New Haven, Conn • Waterville, Maine • London

© 2011 Gale, Cengage Learning

LIBRARY OF CONGRESS CATALOGING-IN-PUBLICATION DATA

Juettner, Bonnie.
  Diet and disease / by Bonnie Juettner.
    p. cm. -- (Nutrition and health)
  Includes bibliographical references and index.
  ISBN 978-1-4205-0269-5 (hardcover)
  1. Nutritionally induced diseases. 2. Nutrition disorders. I. Title.
  RC622.J74 2011
  613.2--dc22
                                                2010035236

Lucent Books
27500 Drake Rd.
Farmington Hills, MI 48331

ISBN-13: 978-1-4205-0269-5
ISBN-10: 1-4205-0269-7

Printed in the United States of America
2 3 4 5 6 7 14 13 12 11

Ptg., 08/2011

TABLE OF CONTENTS

Many people today are often amazed by the amount of nutrition and health information, often contradictory, that can be found in the media. Television, newspapers, and magazines bombard readers with the latest news and recommendations. Television news programs report on recent scientific studies. The healthy living sections of newspapers and magazines offer information and advice. In addition, electronic media such as Web sites, blogs, and forums post daily nutrition and health news and recommendations.

This constant stream of information can be confusing. The science behind nutrition and health is constantly evolving. Current research often leads to new ideas and insights. Many times, the latest nutrition studies and health recommendations contradict previous studies or traditional health advice. When the media report these changes without giving context or explanations, consumers become confused. In a survey by the National Health Council, for example, 68 percent of participants agreed that "when reporting medical and health news, the media often contradict themselves, so I don't know what to believe." In addition, the Food Marketing Institute reported that eight out of ten consumers thought it was likely that nutrition and health experts would have a completely different idea about what foods are healthy within five years. With so much contradictory information, people have difficulty deciding how to apply nutrition and health recommendations to their lives. Students find it difficult to find relevant yet clear and credible information for reports.

Changing recommendations for antioxidant supplements are an example of how confusion can arise. In the 1990s antioxidants, such as vitamins C and E and beta-carotene, came to the public's attention. Scientists found that people who ate more antioxidant-rich foods had a lower risk of heart disease, cancer, vision loss, and other chronic conditions than those who ate lower amounts. Without waiting for more scientific study, the media and supplement companies quickly spread the word that antioxidants could help fight and prevent disease. They recommended that people take antioxidant supplements and eat fortified foods. When further scientific studies were completed, however, most did not support the initial recommendations. While naturally occurring antioxidants in fruits and vegetables may help prevent a variety of chronic diseases, little scientific evidence proved antioxidant supplements had the same effect. In fact, a study published in the November 2008 *Journal of the American Medical Association* found that supplemental vitamins A and C gave no more heart protection than a placebo. The study's results contradicted the widely publicized recommendation, leading to consumer confusion. This example highlights the importance of context for evaluating nutrition and health news. Understanding a topic's scientific background, interpreting a study's findings, and evaluating news sources are critical skills that help reduce confusion.

Lucent's Nutrition and Health series is designed to help young people sift through the mountain of confusing facts, opinions, and recommendations. Each book contains the most up-to-date information, synthesized and written so that students can understand and think critically about nutrition and health issues. Each volume of the series provides a balanced overview of today's hot-button nutrition and health issues while presenting the latest scientific findings and a discussion of issues surrounding the topic. The series provides young people with tools for evaluating conflicting and ever-changing ideas about nutrition and health. Clear narrative peppered with personal anecdotes, fully documented primary and secondary source quotes, informative sidebars, fact boxes, and statistics are all used to help readers understand these topics and how they affect their bodies and their lives. Each volume includes information about changes in trends over time, political controversies, and international perspectives. Full-color photographs and charts enhance all volumes in the series. The Nutrition and Health series is a valuable resource for young people to understand current topics and make informed choices for themselves.

Diet's Impact on Disease

Most Americans die of diseases that doctors classify as highly preventable: heart disease, stroke, most types of cancer, and type 2 diabetes. These diseases are often called the "big four" because they are the four biggest killers of Americans. (Worldwide, most deaths are caused by these four diseases plus respiratory infections.) Doctors say that preventing these diseases requires eating a healthy diet, one that is rich in fruits and vegetables and contains only moderate amounts of lean meat, saturated fat, and processed sugars. Getting plenty of exercise, maintaining a healthy weight, refraining from smoking, and avoiding or restricting alcohol consumption are also essential.

Despite advances in medical research and countless studies demonstrating the value of nutritious food in promoting good health, the US death rate from preventable diseases, especially heart disease, is increasing. Heart disease is the leading cause of death for most Americans. This is especially true among African Americans, whose death rate from heart disease is 30 percent higher than that of whites. Writing in the June 2009 edition of the *American Journal of Medicine*, the journal's editor in chief, Joseph Alpert calls the latest statistics on heart disease "very disturbing" and says that Americans get "failing grades"[1] for their dietary choices.

The average American child, like the average American adult, eats a diet so full of processed sugar and fat and lacking in nutrients that health advocates in the media label it SAD, or the standard American diet. "It's no mistake that the acronym for the Standard American Diet is S.A.D.,"[2] writes chiropractor Jeffrey McCombs in the *Huffington Post*. Pediatrician and children's health writer William Sears agrees, saying, "If you were to list the factors that increase the risk of cancer, heart disease, stroke, intestinal disorders—just about any illness—the standard American diet has them all."[3]

Researchers believe, though, that if people who eat a high-fat, animal-based diet increased their intake of fruits, vegetables, and fiber, obesity rates would drop, degenerative diseases would decrease, and people would live longer. Countless studies have shown that a healthy diet and plenty of exercise make people less susceptible to disease and improve their quality of life. In fact, a 2007 study reported in the *American Journal of Medicine* found that middle-aged American adults who had been eating a poor diet all their lives were able to experience prompt improvements in their health, especially their cardiovascular health, when they began eating a healthy diet. They were much less likely to develop heart disease, and they were also significantly less likely to die in the five years following the study.

People who increase the amount of fruits and vegetables in their diets do more than just improve their immune systems and reduce their risk of chronic diseases. They further improve their overall health by reducing the risk of mood disorders such as depression, according to a 2009 study by the University of Navarra in Spain. Exercise has a similar effect. Medical College of Georgia researchers found that not only does exercise reduce depression, it also improves self-esteem in overweight children who jump rope or play basketball, soccer, or running games.

Through painstaking research, scientists have learned that fruits and vegetables contain much more than vitamins and minerals. Fruits and vegetables also contain phytochemicals, chemicals that benefit the body in numerous ways, including reducing the effects of aging and preventing many kinds of cancer. According to research conducted by molecular biologist Daniel H. Hwang and published by the US Department of Agriculture in April 2009, phytochemicals do this by reducing inflammation in the body. Later in 2009 a University

Countless studies have proven that a diet with increased amounts of fruits and vegetables decreases obesity rates and makes people less susceptible to diseases.

of Florida study showed that phytochemicals also affect human metabolism in ways that make a person less likely to develop obesity and heart disease.

To promote good health, many doctors have begun to encourage their patients to eat a diet based on plants and whole foods (foods that have not been processed or that have been minimally processed—in other words, foods that people cook or prepare for themselves). They encourage their patients to eat a diet that is high in fruits and vegetables, low in meat and saturated fat, and low in sugar. By doing so, people can dramatically reduce their risk of heart disease, stroke, type 2 diabetes, and cancer—all at once.

CHAPTER 1

Four Diseases Diet Could Prevent

Residents and visitors in Chandler, Arizona, can eat at a restaurant called the Heart Attack Grill. The menu contains the following hamburgers: the Double Bypass Burger, the Triple Bypass Burger, and the Quadruple Bypass Burger. The Quadruple Bypass Burger contains 2 pounds (0.9kg) of beef fried in pure lard. The buns are coated in lard, too. The Quadruple Bypass also contains eight slices of cheese. It is an eight-thousand-calorie meal.

The Heart Attack Grill has a sign in the window that reads "Warning: this establishment is BAD for your health."[4] Reporter Bill Geist told CBS News viewers, "From the moment you walk into the place you can almost feel your arteries clogging."[5] The staff of the Heart Attack Grill dress like doctors and nurses. The proprietor calls himself Dr. John and explains that his goal is to provide customers with "taste worth dying for." He continues: "I run perhaps the only honest restaurant in America. Hey, this is bad for you, and it's gonna kill you."[6]

The Big Four Killers

"Dr. John" may be running a gimmick, but according to the experts, he has his facts right. Each meal at his restaurant could well be described as a "heart attack on a plate." The burgers at the Heart Attack Grill are much more extreme than the meals served at most fast-food restaurants, but they share the same basic characteristics: a meal that is high in fat, low in fiber, and low in nutrients. According to doctors, eating a diet that is too much like the food served at the Heart Attack Grill is causing three out of four Americans to die early from cancer, stroke, type 2 diabetes, and most of all, heart disease.

These four types of disease are the four biggest killers of Americans. They are also highly preventable through diet. Research has shown that a healthy diet can help prevent the diseases that are most likely to cause death. On the other hand, an unhealthy diet—one that is high in fat and calories and low in fiber and essential nutrients—can set a person up for conditions such as cardiovascular disease and obesity that contribute to these big four killers.

Cardiovascular disease refers to disease affecting the heart and blood vessels. An unhealthy diet can lead to a buildup of plaque—fat, cholesterol, and other substances—inside the

The Heart Attack Grill's Triple Bypass Burger is advertised as hazardous to your health.

arteries. This buildup of plaque can cause the walls of the arteries to narrow and become thick and irregular, which reduces blood flow and can lead to cardiovascular disease. According to the American Heart Association, one in three American adults has some form of cardiovascular disease, and it is the leading cause of death in America and around the world. About twenty-three hundred Americans die of cardiovascular disease every day—on average, one every thirty-eight seconds. The most common forms of cardiovascular disease are heart disease and stroke.

Heart Disease

According to the Centers for Disease Control and Prevention, heart disease claimed the lives of 631,636 Americans in 2006. It is responsible for approximately half of all deaths each year. Heart disease includes both heart attack and heart failure.

Approximately 5.7 million Americans are currently living with heart failure, according to the American Heart Association. Heart failure is a serious long-term condition that occurs when the heart cannot keep up with its workload. The heart becomes progressively weaker over time, until finally it cannot pump enough blood to bring needed oxygen and nutrients to tissues in the body. In 2006 almost one out of every nine death certificates listed heart failure as the cause of death. Another one out of every six deaths that year were caused by coronary artery disease, which occurs when the blood vessels of the heart narrow and become congested, leading to a heart attack. Coronary artery disease is usually caused by atherosclerosis, the buildup of fatty deposits and plaque in the arteries. About once every twenty-five seconds an American has a heart attack, and about once every minute someone will die of one.

Heart attacks occur when the blood flow to the heart (or a section of the heart) becomes blocked, again due to a buildup of plaque in the arteries. A section of plaque can

NUTRITION FACT

33 grams

The average American consumes about 33 grams, or 297 calories, of saturated fat each day.

Three Percent of Americans Have Healthy Lifestyles

American doctors, especially cardiologists, have been studying the relationship between nutrition and disease for years—and for just as many years, they have been worrying about how the American diet will affect people's health. A study conducted in 2005 at Michigan State University found that only 3 percent of American adults are able to do all four of the following: eat a healthy diet, maintain a healthy weight, exercise regularly, and refrain from smoking. Fewer than one-quarter of American adults ate a diet that researchers considered healthy (one that was rich in fruits and vegetables), and a little over one-third managed to maintain a healthy weight.

Follow-up studies published in January 2007 and March 2009 showed that the diets of American youths are equally unhealthy. The 2007 study, which was conducted by researchers from the University of Minnesota, showed that teens eat fewer fruits and vegetables as they get older. The 2009 study, in which researchers from Ohio State University analyzed the results of a national nutrition survey, showed that not only did children not eat the recommended number of servings of fruits and vegetables, but about 46 percent of the vegetables children did eat were potatoes. Only 8 percent of the vegetables eaten by children and teens are dark green or orange—colors associated with vitamins and minerals that growing bodies need in their diets.

Quoted in Katrina Woznicki, "Few Americans Following 'Big Four' Healthy Lifestyle," *MedPage Today,* April 27, 2005. www.medpagetoday.com/PrimaryCare/Exercise Fitness/948.

A nutritionist counsels a heart patient about proper eating habits. Proper diet is a key factor in fighting heart disease.

rupture and cause a blood clot to form inside an artery. This clot can block the flow of blood to a section of heart muscle. If the blood flow is not quickly restored, the section of heart muscle that is deprived of oxygen begins to die.

Because heart disease causes such serious health complications and is so widespread, many cardiologists consider it to be the biggest medical challenge facing the United States today. The National Heart, Lung, and Blood Institute offers a list of ways people can reduce their risk of heart disease and specifically heart attack. This list includes not smoking, reducing or eliminating alcohol consumption, losing excess weight, exercising, and following a healthy diet that includes foods low in calories, fat, and sodium.

Stroke

Cardiovascular disease can do more than cause heart failure or a heart attack. It can also cause a stroke, a disorder that some people call a "brain attack." A stroke occurs when an artery leading to the brain, rather than the heart, becomes blocked with fatty deposits and plaque, or when a blood vessel in the brain bursts or is clogged by a blood clot. Just as with heart tissue, when brain tissue is starved for oxygen for too long, it begins to die. Strokes are the third leading cause of death in the United States, killing about 137,000 Americans every year. Those who survive a stroke may be left with brain damage, which can impair behavior or body functions.

Studies show that lifestyle choices such as eating a nutritious diet, getting plenty of exercise, refraining from smoking, and keeping alcohol use moderate can cut a person's risk of stroke in half. The Mayo Clinic lists many steps people can take to reduce their risk of stroke. These include controlling cholesterol levels and blood pressure by eating a healthy diet, maintaining a healthy weight, and exercising regularly. Losing as little as 10 pounds (4.5kg) may lower blood pressure and improve cholesterol levels, according to the Mayo Clinic.

Maintaining a healthy weight is especially important in the prevention of strokes because being overweight can contribute to other risk factors for stroke, such as cardiovascu-

The chart below shows the number of deaths from heart disease, cancer, stroke, and diabetes in the United States for 2007, the most recent year for which data is available.

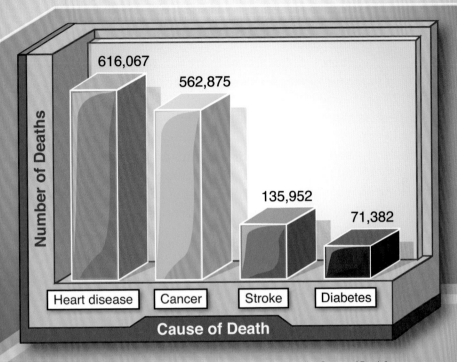

616,067

562,875

135,952

71,382

Number of Deaths

Heart disease | Cancer | Stroke | Diabetes

Cause of Death

Taken from: Centers for Disease Control and Prevention, "Leading Causes of Death." www.cdc.gov/nchs/fastats/lcod.htm.

lar disease, high blood pressure, and diabetes. In addition, obesity, especially abdominal obesity—extra fat around the waistline—has been found to increase a person's risk of having a stroke. In 2002 researchers managed to quantify the relationship between excess weight and risk of stroke. For every 6 to 7 pounds (2.7 to 3.2kg) that a man gains, his risk of stroke increases by 6 percent. Researchers are not certain why increased abdominal fat also increases the risk of stroke, but they think it is probably because people who have a large waist circumference also tend to have high blood pressure and/or diabetes—both of which are also known risk factors for stroke.

Obesity

Obesity is not only a risk factor for stroke; it is a primary connection between diet and many other diseases. Late in 2009 researchers announced that obesity had become a bigger threat to life expectancy than smoking. John McMurray, professor of cardiology at the Western Infirmary in Glasgow, Scotland, says: "Obesity is at least as great a risk factor for heart failure as it is for heart attack or stroke. Obesity more than doubles the risk."[7] Scientists are not yet sure why obesity increases the risk of heart failure so dramatically. They do know that obesity requires the heart to work harder and can cause changes to the structure of the heart, such as increasing its size.

Obesity increases a person's risk of not only heart disease and stroke but also diabetes and cancer—in other words, all of the big four killers. About two-thirds of Americans, including about 17 percent of children between the ages of six and eleven and 18 percent of teenagers, are considered

Obesity is not only directly connected to many diseases, it is also a risk factor for strokes.

overweight or obese, according to current medical guidelines. A person who is more than 10 percent above his or her ideal body weight is considered overweight, whereas someone who is more than 20 percent above his or her ideal body weight is considered obese.

Because obesity increases the body's mass, the body has to work harder. All the body's systems have more work, but the heart bears the brunt of the added workload. The heart must pump blood to a larger area. When the heart cannot keep up with its workload, it does not just stop working. Instead, the body reacts in other ways. First the heart builds itself up, becoming larger and more muscular so that it can contract more strongly. The left side of the heart, in particular, tends to become larger and thicker. This is not a good situation, says cardiologist Desiree Dizadji. She explains that the heart is "not like a muscle where bigger might be better. It puts more strain on the heart (the heart is an organ too, and needs its own blood flow and nutrients) and causes the heart to perform as a pump in a less effective way."[8]

> ## NUTRITION FACT
> ### 12 teaspoons
> The average American consumes more than twelve teaspoons of sugar per day (not counting the sugar that is in fruit).

Over the last twenty years, the number of children and teens with abnormally thick hearts has nearly doubled. "The obesity epidemic is indeed having adverse effects on the hearts of children," says David Crowley, a cardiologist at Cincinnati Children's Hospital. "If we do not get a handle on this in this country, if kids continue to get heavier, their hearts will inevitably get thicker and kids will be at higher risk of heart attacks and strokes."[9]

In obese children and adults, the heart also reacts to its extra workload—having a larger area to pump blood to—by pumping faster. The body reacts in other ways, too. Blood vessels become narrower to keep blood pressure up and cause blood to move more vigorously through the body, and the body sends less blood to less important tissues so that it can send more blood to its most essential organs—the heart and the brain.

Obesity and the diseases that often go with it can be the result of eating a diet that is high in junk food. Junk food is a term that refers to foods that are dense in calories but low in nutrients. These foods consist mostly of what nutritionists and dieticians call "empty calories," calories that offer the body sugar energy and not much more. Junk food includes soda, chips, fast food, fried food, candy, energy drinks, and the like. Studies show that Americans get almost one-third of their calories from junk food.

Type 2 Diabetes

Poor dietary choices, such as eating too much junk food, not only cause weight gain but also make a person much more likely to develop type 2 diabetes. In people with type 2 diabetes, glucose (sugar) builds up in the blood instead of going into the body's cells, which prevents the cells from functioning properly. Doctors say that obesity is the biggest risk factor for diabetes. According to a 2009 study headed by Elbert S. Huang of the University of Chicago, the total number of Americans with diabetes will rise from 23.7 million to 44.1 million over the next twenty-five years. Another 2009 study, conducted by lead researcher Supriya Krishnan of the Harvard School of Public Health, found that type 2 diabetes rates for African American women are highest among those who eat a lot of restaurant food, especially fried chicken, fried fish, hamburgers, and Chinese food. Krishnan's team of researchers concluded that this type of diet is a risk factor for type 2 diabetes.

Over time, a junk food diet can lead to diabetes by changing the chemical balance in the blood. In a healthy person, the body responds to sugar intake by producing a hormone called insulin, which helps sugar to move from the blood into the body's cells, where it can be used as fuel. When people eat a diet that is high in sugar, the body repeatedly releases large amounts of insulin to control all the sugar that is released into the blood. When the body is frequently exposed to an excessive amount of insulin, it can develop insulin resistance, a condition in which the body's cells have become used to the presence of insulin and do not respond to it as much as they should.

As a result of insulin resistance, the body must compensate by producing more insulin. Insulin resistance is a precursor to type 2 diabetes, the most common form of the disease. In people with type 2 diabetes, either the body does not produce enough insulin, or the body does not respond properly to the insulin that it does produce. Diabetes is a very serious disease that can cause nerve damage, high blood pressure, and arterial disease. Diabetes, therefore, can be another risk factor for the development of heart disease or stroke. The Harvard School of Public Health points out that type 2 diabetes is highly preventable through abstaining from smoking and alcohol, maintaining a healthy weight, getting enough physical activity, and eating a proper diet, including whole grains and healthy fats.

Eating too much fried food can cause weight gain and make a person more susceptible to developing type 2 diabetes.

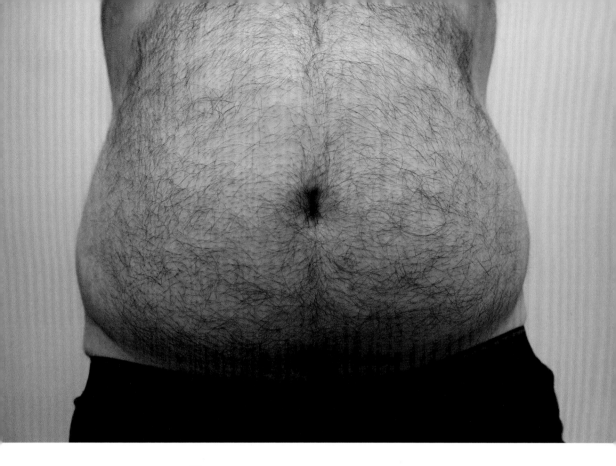

Researchers have concluded that excessive body fat may be the cause of 49 percent of endometrial cancer, 35 percent of esophageal cancer, 24 percent of kidney cancer, 21 percent of gall bladder cancers, and 17 percent of breast cancer.

Cancer

Cancer, too, is often linked to the same factors that cause cardiovascular disease and diabetes. According to the National Cancer Institute, scientists believe that about 14 percent of men and 20 percent of women who die from cancer had cancers that were related to their obesity. Late in 2009 researchers with the American Institute for Cancer Research released a study breaking down the numbers for overweight-related cancers according to the type of cancer. Excess body fat, researchers concluded, may be the cause of 49 percent of endometrial cancers, 35 percent of esophageal cancer, 24 percent of kidney cancer, 21 percent of gall-bladder cancer, 17 percent of breast cancer, and 9 percent of colorectal cancer. Why obesity raises the risk of developing certain cancers is not yet known. Scientists think that fat cells have the ability to alter blood chemistry in ways that lead to the development of cancer. For example, fat cells are thought to release hormones, which can lead to certain cancers. Yet whether excess fat is a direct cause of these cancers has yet to be proved.

Eating a diet high in fruits and vegetables is a well-known and very effective method of preventing many kinds of cancer. Researchers have found that fruits and vegetables contain chemicals that help reduce inflammation in the body, which can help reduce a person's risk for many diseases, including cancer. This link between a diet high in fruits and vegetables and a decreased cancer risk was demonstrated by a study published in the journal *Pharmaceutical Research* in July 2008. The study noted that people who become obese often eat a diet that is rich in meat, fat, dairy products, and sugar but low in fruits and vegetables. Consequently, they are less likely to get the foods that they need in their diets in order to prevent cancer. While not eating the fruits and vegetables that might protect them from cancer, many overweight and obese people are instead consuming foods that are known to be linked to the development of cancer, such as fried food, red meat, and alcohol, all of which lead to chronic inflammation in the body.

Diseases Working Together

Any one of the four chronic diseases that kill Americans can be a major health problem all by itself. However, for a person to have more than one of these diseases is not unusual because the same factors that can lead to one disease—for example, too much fat around the waist, high blood pressure, and high blood sugar—can also lead to the others. For this reason, a person who has one of these four major diseases is at increased risk of developing any of the other three. In addition, heart disease, stroke, type 2 diabetes, and cancer are all associated with obesity, so obese people often develop more than one of these diseases.

When the same person has more than one disease, the combined effects of the diseases have an even greater impact on the person's health. For example, in June 2009 the European Society of Cardiology presented the results of a large European survey of heart patients at the Heart Failure

Think More About It: Life Expectancy

Many people have the misconception that dying of heart disease is just another way to die of old age. The fact is that 32 percent of people who die of heart disease are younger than age seventy-five when they die. Some are quite a few years younger. In 2005 the average American's life expectancy hit a new high: nearly seventy-eight years, which is among the highest life expectancies of any country in the world. The change was due to decreases in deaths from chronic diseases such as heart disease, cancer, and stroke, according to survey statistician Hsiang-Ching Kung of the Centers for Disease Control and Prevention. If more Americans changed their lifestyles and the amount of heart disease in the nation was reduced, the average American's life expectancy would rise still further.

According to the National Center for Health Statistics, if cardiovascular disease in all its major forms could be eliminated, the average American's life expectancy would rise by almost five years. Twenty other countries have lower rates of heart disease than the United States, and in those countries, which include Japan and several Mediterranean countries, life expectancies are higher as well.

Congress in Nice, France. The 2009 study showed that obesity and diabetes (together or separately) greatly increase a patient's risk of heart failure. Like obesity, type 2 diabetes doubles the risk of heart failure in patients. In addition, diabetics who develop heart disease have worse symptoms, are more likely to be hospitalized, and are more likely to die of heart failure. Heart disease and type 2 diabetes are so closely intertwined that scientists are not certain whether diabetes increases the risk of heart disease or whether heart disease increases the risk of diabetes. "Whichever is the causative factor," says McMurray, "it's very bad news for those with both conditions."[10]

The good news, though, is that simple dietary changes can prevent most cases of heart disease, type 2 diabetes, stroke, and cancer. Today, doctors, nutritionists, and others who specialize in diet have confirmed the words of Hippocrates, the ancient Greek doctor, who once said, "Let food be thy medicine; thy medicine shall be thy food."[11] The best diet, these experts say, can be described in a nutshell: Eat more plants, less meat, and less junk food.

CHAPTER 2

Diet and Deficiencies

Even though humans can be very flexible about diet, they still need certain nutrients in order to live and to avoid disease. When people do not get the nutrients they need in their diet, their bodies get out of balance, which means that instead of having the right amount of each nutrient, they have too little of some nutrients and too much of others. This can lead to malnutrition, a condition that can result from an inadequate or imbalanced diet. If a nutritional imbalance or deficiency is minor, it might not even be noticed. Over time, however, an unbalanced or deficient diet can contribute to the development of a disorder, or it can weaken the body so that it succumbs more easily to diseases. In some cases, a deficiency can lead to malnutrition so severe that the person may suffer irreversible damage and even death.

The human body, however, is very resilient and is able to survive under a variety of conditions, including not getting optimum nutrition. One reason humans are so resilient is that the body's cells can make most, but not all, of the substances that they need from a few raw materials. Sometimes these basic raw materials that the body needs are called macronutrients, because *macro* means "large," and the body needs large amounts of these nutrients. The two most basic materials that the cells need are the elements carbon and nitrogen. The body's cells can make carbon from sugar and nitrogen from protein. Sugar and protein are in almost every kind of food, which is why humans can, if they have to, survive on all sorts of different diets. Merely staying alive, however, is far different from getting all the nutrients needed to be healthy and to ward off disease.

Carbohydrates

Nutritionists recommend that carbohydrates—foods that provide people with energy—make up the largest part of the diet. Carbohydrates include foods that provide sugars, starches, and

A selection of foods that contain carbohydrates. Nutritionists recommend that carbohydrates make up the largest part of one's diet.

fiber. Carbohydrates are made by plants—which nutritionists also say should form the basis of a healthy diet. Fruits, vegetables, and whole grains are healthy sources of carbohydrates.

Carbohydrates supply energy in the form of glucose, a type of sugar, to the whole body. The brain uses more glucose, though, than any other organ. More than 60 percent of the glucose in the blood is used by the brain. This is one reason carbohydrates are so vital to good health.

Although having carbohydrates in the diet is important, not all carbohydrates are equally nutritious. Dieticians say that humans need carbohydrates that come from whole foods, such as whole grains, fruits, and vegetables. Many carbohydrates are refined, which means they are produced by taking one part of a plant and throwing away the rest. This is done to give foods a finer texture and to prolong the shelf life of food products. Refined carbohydrates can still supply energy to the brain. Nutritionally, however, refined carbohydrates create two problems.

First, when a carbohydrate is refined, such as when wheat is processed into white flour to make white bread, the parts of the plant that are thrown away often contain important vitamins, minerals, fiber, and other nutrients that the human body needs. Second, because they are readily digestible, refined carbohydrates cause blood sugar levels to spike suddenly, which causes insulin levels to surge in response and increases the likelihood that a person will become insulin resistant. This process can contribute to the development of diabetes.

Whole foods, on the other hand, tend to release sugar gradually into the bloodstream. Steady, even blood sugar levels are better for the brain. A steady supply of sugar means that the brain will have enough fuel, but not too much—too much glucose can cause nerve damage (which is one of the side effects of diabetes). This is because glucose molecules are very large and can block the flow of blood through the body's smallest blood vessels, such as those in the nerves, which can eventually become damaged.

NUTRITION FACT

18 Percent

The average restaurant meal contains 18 percent more calories than is indicated on the menu.

Fiber

In addition to supplying the body with energy, carbohydrates also supply another essential nutrient: fiber. Fiber is the part of the plant that the human body cannot digest. Humans need two kinds of fiber in their diet— soluble and insoluble. Oddly enough, the very fact that humans cannot digest fiber is what makes it so helpful.

Soluble fiber is fiber that dissolves in water. This type of fiber is found in oats, beans, and fruits, especially apples. It is absorbed by the body and, even though it is not digested,

Soluble fiber is found in oats, beans, and fruit and is important because it lowers high cholesterol and prevents constipation.

passes into the blood. Soluble fiber can prevent constipation because when it combines with stool, this fiber helps to hold water in, keeping stool soft so that it can pass through the intestines easily. Because soluble fiber binds with cholesterol and carries it out of the body, a lack of this type of fiber can contribute to high cholesterol levels and increase the risk of heart disease. Insufficient soluble fiber also contributes to the development of gallstones, which can form from an excess of cholesterol in the gallbladder.

Insoluble fiber, as its name implies, does not dissolve in water. Because it cannot be digested, it is not absorbed by the body but instead moves through the intestines, pushing stool along and scraping the walls of the intestines clean. By pushing food through the intestines, insoluble fiber helps the body eliminate waste and toxins that would otherwise build up in the intestines and elsewhere in the body. A diet that lacks sufficient insoluble fiber can lead to problems such as constipation, headaches, fatigue, acne, and eczema. It can also lead to more serious conditions, such as irritable bowel syndrome, and can even contribute to colon cancer.

The total intake of both kinds of fiber is also important. Fiber affects blood chemistry by helping to regulate levels of sugar and fat in the blood, keeping them from getting too high. A diet that is low in total fiber can contribute to hypoglycemia (low blood sugar) and diabetes. Heart disease, prostate cancer, and breast cancer have also been linked to a diet that contains too little fiber.

Protein

The body needs carbohydrates to supply energy and fiber. It also needs amino acids to grow and maintain new cells and tissues and to keep the brain and nervous system healthy. One of the most common forms of malnutrition worldwide is an amino acid deficiency. Amino acids are the molecules, or building blocks, that make up protein. Humans need twenty different amino acids, and all but eight of those can be made by the body's cells as long as the diet includes protein. The remaining eight amino acids that the body cannot make on its own are called the essential amino acids. Animal

products, such as meat, eggs, and dairy products, contain all eight essential amino acids. Plants also contain the essential amino acids, but not all eight at once, so vegans (people who do not eat meat, eggs, or dairy products) must eat a variety of plants in order to get all the amino acids they need.

Dairy products and eggs contain the eight essential amino acids the body cannot make on its own.

All foods contain some amino acids, so almost anyone who gets enough to eat will have enough protein. One out of six people worldwide, however, do not get enough to eat and have a protein deficiency. When children do not get enough protein, their growth is stunted and their brains do not develop properly. This can result in further problems such as learning disabilities and, frequently, behavior problems. "Nutritional deprivation leaves children tired and weak, and lowers their IQs, so they perform poorly in school,"[12] explains Ann Veneman, the executive director of the United Nations Children's Fund.

In 2008, 65 percent of people who were protein-deficient lived in seven countries: India, China, the Democratic Republic of the Congo, Bangladesh, Indonesia, Pakistan, and Ethiopia. Even in developed countries such as the United States, 21 percent of families go hungry some of the time. Children who are undernourished, even for a day, are not likely to perform well in school that day. Children who do not regularly get enough to eat frequently have difficulty paying attention in school. In addition, a severe protein deficiency can lead to wasting away of the body's tissues, can inhibit a child's growth and proper development, and can result in poor healing of wounds. Protein deficiencies have been linked to such serious diseases as heart disease, breast cancer, colon cancer, and osteoporosis (a decrease in bone density).

Fat

Keeping the body healthy requires more than glucose and fiber from carbohydrates and amino acids from protein. It also requires that the diet contain a healthy amount of fat. Even people who think they have plenty of fat on their own bodies need to include at least some fat in their diet. The body uses fat to build cell membranes (the outside layer, or skin, of each cell) and to make certain hormones. The body also uses fat to carry certain vitamins, such as vitamins A, D, E, and K, into the body. Vitamins A, D, E, and K are called fat-soluble vitamins because they can be dissolved and stored in fat.

Although fat is used by the whole body, it is most important for the health of the nervous system and the brain. If all the water was taken out of a human brain, what was left would be 60 percent fat—and the sheath that is wrapped around every nerve cell in the body is made out of 75 percent fat. The body needs a sufficient intake of fat in order for the brain to develop and function properly.

Insufficient fat in the diet can lead to problems elsewhere in the body, too, including hair loss, a lack of luster and sheen in the hair, and nails that are too brittle or too hard. Because fats make up part of all body cells, people with insufficient fat in their diets can have difficulty in maintaining their normal body temperature.

Fat is either saturated or unsaturated. Saturated fat—or "bad" fat—is a kind of fat that usually becomes solid at room temperature. Saturated fats are the kind of fats that are in meat, butter, cheese, whole milk, ice cream, cream, and some tropical vegetable oils. Saturated fats increase the risk of heart attacks, strokes, and several kinds of cancer.

Unsaturated vegetable fat is better for heart health than saturated fat. It is often called "good" fat. Unsaturated vegetable fat includes the fat in olives (and olive oil), avocados, and most nuts. Like saturated fats, though, vegetable fats improve the taste of foods and help a person to feel full. They also promote weight gain and obesity—so even though they are classified as good fats, they still must be eaten in moderation.

Unsaturated fats are not all alike. Some saturated fats are more important than others. Two of the most important are omega-6 and omega-3, known as the essential fatty acids. They are called essential because they are absolutely necessary for good health and because they are one kind of fat that human bodies do not make on their own. They are also essential because they reduce inflammation (the redness and irritation that occur when tissue is damaged), control blood clotting, and are used by the brain to make connections between nerves. Also, including healthy fats in a meal slows down digestion, helping people to feel full sooner and to be able to go for longer periods of time without getting hungry again. In this way, including fat in the diet can be a good strategy for maintaining a healthy weight. At the same time, though, the amount of fat the body needs is small. The Food and Drug Administration recommends people aged four and older get only about 2.3 ounces (65g) of fat a day.

NUTRITION FACT

8 Percent

The average frozen meal purchased from a supermarket contains 8 percent more calories than indicated on the label.

Vitamins and Minerals

In addition to carbohydrates, protein, and fat, the human body needs other nutrients that the body cannot make for itself—nutrients such as vitamins and minerals that can only come from fruits and vegetables. Like amino acids, vitamins are molecules—but unlike amino acids, the body needs only small amounts of each vitamin. Minerals are elements such as iron, calcium, and magnesium. Vitamins and minerals are sometimes called micronutrients. The body needs only tiny, trace amounts of vitamins and minerals, but it cannot function properly without them. When the body does not get enough of the vitamins or minerals it needs, various deficiencies can result.

The most common vitamin and mineral deficiency worldwide is iron deficiency, which causes anemia. (A vitamin B_{12} deficiency, which is common among vegetarians, can also cause anemia.) The body uses iron to make hemoglobin, a protein in the blood that carries oxygen to the body's various cells and tissues. If the body's cells do not get enough oxygen, a person can start to feel weak, cold, dizzy, or irritable. Anemia also increases a person's likelihood of dying from heart failure, because heart tissue needs oxygen just as much as the other tissues in the body do.

Simply eating iron-rich foods is not enough to ensure that a person will not be anemic. The iron in the foods must be absorbed in the intestines or it will pass out of the body unused. The intestines do not absorb iron well when it is alone, however. In order for iron to pass into the body's cells, vitamin C must be present, too. Eating red meat every night for dinner by itself is therefore not enough to guard against anemia. It may be necessary to eat oranges, broccoli, or another good source of vitamin C along with it. Iron and vitamin C should be paired together to ensure the iron is absorbed.

Vitamin A Deficiency

Another common deficiency is vitamin A deficiency (VAD). Worldwide, 33 percent of children under the age of five are believed to be suffering from VAD. Preschoolers who do not get enough vitamin A are 23 percent more likely to die from common diseases such as measles, diarrhea, and malaria. Vitamin A–deficient children who survive those diseases often end up going blind. Milder VAD is connected with vision impairment.

Good dietary sources of vitamin A include liver and various vegetables such as carrots, sweet potatoes, pumpkins, broccoli, kale, and spinach. Like iron, vitamin A is not

Vitamin Deficiency Diseases

New York Times columnist Nicholas Kristof, returning from a trip to Honduras in 2010, wrote about the vitamin deficiency disease he observed in a Tegucigalpa hospital. In the hospital, Kristof met Rosa Alvarez, an eighteen-day-old baby who had just had surgery to repair a hole in her spine. He met Angel Flores, who had soft tissue sticking out of his back. He met Jose Tercera, whose mother unwrapped a bandage around his head to show Kristof the golf-ball-size chunk of his brain that was extending out through a hole in Tercera's forehead.

The spinal and skull deformities that Kristof observed are called neural tube defects. They occurred before these children were born. Neural tube defects are completely preventable if pregnant mothers eat a diet that is rich in micronutrients such as vitamins and minerals, especially vitamin B9, or folic acid.

Pregnancy and early childhood (the years from birth to age five) are the time in a human's life when good nutrition matters the most. In addition to the B vitamins, children have a strong need for iodine, iron, zinc, and vitamin A. A lack of iodine in the diet can lead to thyroid disorders, whereas insufficient iron can lead to anemia. A lack of zinc and vitamin A can weaken the immune system and increase the number of deaths from infections and diarrhea.

Neural tube defects are spinal and skull deformities brought about by a mother's lack of vitamins and minerals during pregnancy.

absorbed well unless it is paired with another nutrient—in this case, fat. Vitamin A is fat soluble, not water soluble—it will dissolve only in fat, not water. The body cannot pick up vitamin A from the intestines unless it has fat in which to dissolve the vitamin A, so fat needs to be present in order for the vitamin to travel through the blood to the parts of the body that need it.

Vitamin D Deficiency

Vitamin D is made in the skin in response to sunlight. It can also be found in fish, eggs, fortified milk, and cod liver oil. Vitamin D helps the body to absorb calcium. It also helps the body to absorb phosphorus, another mineral that is important in bone formation. Children who do not get enough vitamin D can develop rickets, a disease that causes the skeleton to become malformed.

In 2009 scientists made a breakthrough in their research on vitamin D. They learned that in addition to being critical for bone health, vitamin D is also important for the immune system, the lungs, and cardiovascular health. Late in 2009 researchers at the Heart Institute at Intermountain Medical Center in Salt Lake City, Utah, released a

Fish and eggs are good sources of vitamin D, which helps the body absorb calcium and phosphorus, two essential minerals in bone formation.

study showing that insufficient levels of vitamin D in the body has a strong effect on a person's risk of heart disease, stroke, and death. The study followed almost thirty thousand people over the age of fifty who had no history of heart disease. People with low vitamin D levels were twice as likely, during the year or so that the study lasted, to develop heart failure, 77 percent more likely to die, 45 percent more likely to develop coronary artery disease, and 78 percent more likely to have a stroke than people with normal vitamin D levels.

A different 2009 study led by Jared P. Reis, a postdoctoral research fellow at Johns Hopkins Bloomberg School of Public Health in Baltimore, Maryland, showed that even in teenagers, low vitamin D levels more than doubled the risk of high blood pressure and high blood sugar and nearly quadrupled the risk of obesity. About 70 percent of American children and teens are believed to be vitamin D deficient. Michal Melamed, a professor at the Albert Einstein School of Medicine in New York City, conducted a study in 2009 that looked at vitamin D levels in the blood of six thousand people under the age of twenty-one. Nine percent of the children in the study were clinically deficient in vitamin D, and another 61 percent had such low levels of vitamin D in their blood that they were at high risk for deficiency. In the United States, African American and Latino children are at the highest risk for vitamin D deficiency—80 percent of Latino children and 92 percent of African American children are not getting enough vitamin D.

Children with deficient or nearly deficient levels of vitamin D are more likely to catch cold and flu viruses, more likely to develop pneumonia, and more likely to develop winter-related eczema. They also have higher blood pressure and weaker bones than children who are not deficient. Melamed commented: "Adults with low vitamin-D levels

NUTRITION FACT

1 billion

More than 1 billion people regularly went hungry in 2009. Worldwide, the most common diet-related disorder is malnutrition caused by starvation.

are at risk for diabetes, high blood pressure, cardiovascular disease, and a lot of cancers, and if kids start out with low levels and never increase them, they may be putting themselves at risk for developing all of these diseases at a much earlier age."[13]

Nutrients out of Balance

Vitamin D deficiency is but one example of how low levels of just one nutrient can have a dramatic effect on the human body. Vitamin D deficiency is also an example of how a vitamin deficiency can cause a disease to develop so slowly that people may be unaware of it. People who are deficient in vitamin D and other vitamins may still function normally in their daily lives—especially if the deficiency is not severe.

Over time, though, a vitamin deficiency can contribute to the gradual deterioration of certain tissues. For example, one of the reasons people tend to develop memory problems and sometimes dementia—a memory, concentration, and judgment impairment—as they age is that older people are more likely to have a vitamin B_{12} deficiency. Research released by Oxford University in 2008 showed that the brain shrinks more with age in people who are vitamin B_{12} deficient.

In addition to preventing the body from developing an imbalance, vitamins and minerals also help to strengthen the immune system. While some kinds of disorders are caused by nutritional imbalances, others are caused by a pathogen, such as a germ, when it enters the body. Germs can enter the body in several ways: by being breathed in through the respiratory system; by being ingested in food or drink through the digestive system; or through openings in the skin, such as wounds that may become infected. When the body is healthy and strong,

NUTRITION FACT

Vitamin A was not discovered until 1913, but traditional doctors have long prescribed foods that happen to be rich in vitamin A as a remedy for vision problems. For example, as far back as the fifth century B.C., Hippocrates prescribed liver, a good source of vitamin A, for night blindness.

Top Ten Essential Vitamins and Minerals

The following is a list of the top ten essential vitamins and minerals, good sources for each, and the importance of each.

Vitamins	Good Sources	Important for . . .
Vitamin B Complex	Meat, liver, milk, yeast, nuts, whole grain cereals	Helps body's energy production, nervous system, immune system, iron absorption
Vitamin C	Kiwi and citrus fruits, guava, mango, broccoli	Helps in formation of enzymes, absorption of iron, antioxidant function, formation of collagen, wound healing
Vitamin D	Cod liver oil, milk, eggs, liver, oily fish	Bone formation
Vitamin E	Wheat germ oil, almonds, sunflower oil, peanuts	Protects tissue from free-radical damage, improves blood circulation, healing wounds and scars
Vitamin K	Spinach, broccoli, eggs, meat	Blood clotting

Minerals

Calcium	Dairy products, almonds, beans, sesame seeds, broccoli	Bone and teeth formation, nervous system health
Iron	Eggs, meat, liver, fish	Red blood cell formation
Potassium	Beans, potatoes, sweet potatoes, bananas, dried fruits, winter squash, cantaloupe, kiwi, avocados	Maintain healthy blood pressure, reduce risk of stroke
Selenium	Sunflower seeds, fish, shellfish, red meat, Brazil nuts	Supports immune system, reduces inflammation
Zinc	Meat, vegetables with leaves, whole grains, milk, eggs	Growth and development, immune function, wound healing

Taken from: Tamer Shaban, "Your Guide to Essential Vitamins and Minerals," *Natural News,* May 7, 2008. www.naturalnews.com/023182_vitamins_deficiency_natural.html. Ygoy.com, "10 Important Vitamins and Minerals Your Body Needs," July 23, 2007. http://vitamins.ygoy.com/2007/07/23/10-important-vitamins-and-minerals-body-needs.

Recovering from Anorexia

Some American teens are malnourished because they eat foods that lack nutrition value. Others are malnourished because they eat almost nothing at all. Forty-year-old Sherri Crowl of Edinboro, Pennsylvania, was anorexic for twenty-two years—all of her teenage and young adult years, and even part of her childhood. Looking back on her experience, she remembers: "I'd eat one meal a week if I had to . . . my eating disorder started when I was eight. . . . I kept thinking, if I could be thinner, people would be in awe of me and want to be that size too."

When she turned thirty, Crowl was finally diagnosed with anorexia, a mental disorder that causes its victims to starve themselves deliberately as they try to get thinner and thinner. Anorexics may think that being thinner is healthier, but starvation is not healthy—it deprives the body of nutrients that it needs. For teenagers, anorexia can deprive the body of nutrients that are needed in order for the body to grow taller or for the brain to continue its development.

At the worst phase of Crowl's disease, she was living mostly on gum and tea. She would spend hours every day running on a treadmill. When she finally got help, the doctor who examined her said that her heart was beating so slowly that if she had not gotten treatment, she would have been dead within a month.

Quoted in Kathleen Phalen Tomaselli, "Starving for Perfection: The Changing Face of Anorexia," *American Medical News*, May 5, 2008, p. 27.

Anorexia is a mental disorder that causes its victims to deliberately starve themselves as they try to get thinner and thinner.

it can defend itself much more vigorously against germs, so a person gets well faster or may not become sick at all.

Having their nutrients out of balance is a risk for three-quarters of Americans, including children and teenagers, who do not eat the recommended amounts of fruits and vegetables every day. Most do not get enough whole grains, either. The diets of three-quarters of Americans are particularly low in dark green leafy vegetables, orange vegetables, and legumes. In 2009 the Centers for Disease Control and Prevention estimated that only 14 percent of adults and fewer than 10 percent of teenagers in the United States eat three servings of vegetables and two servings of fruit every day. The human body is flexible and resilient. It does not need each nutrient to be supplied in an exact amount. It does, however, need nutrients to stay within certain general ranges.

Keeping track of vitamins and minerals, fat and fiber, and amino acids and protein in the diet may seem very complicated. It is not necessary, however, for people to track every nutrient that they receive or to figure out whether they are getting enough of each vitamin and mineral. Nutritionists say that if people eat a plant-based diet—including a wide variety of fruits, vegetables, and whole grains—and moderate amounts of meat, sugar, and fat, then they will get most of the nutrients that they need without even trying.

CHAPTER 3

How Diet Can Prevent Disease

A healthy diet can help prevent many diseases, including cardiovascular disease, diabetes, and certain cancers. Eating the right amount of healthy foods can also help control some conditions such as obesity, high blood pressure, and high cholesterol levels. Numerous studies have shown the health benefits of eating more fruits and vegetables. For example, a 2007 study published in the *American Journal of Medicine* followed fifteen thousand people for more than twenty years. The study examined the participants' lifestyle habits, including diet, exercise, weight, and smoking. The authors of the study reported that those people who ate five servings of fruits and vegetables a day, exercised regularly, controlled their weight, and refrained from smoking were 35 percent less likely to develop heart disease and 40 percent less likely to die during a four-year-period following the study than those who did not follow these lifestyle habits.

Other studies have shown that a diet that includes plenty of fruits and vegetables and limits meats (especially fatty meats), fats, calories, and alcohol can help prevent many diseases. One of the most widely touted diets in recent years, the Mediterranean diet, combines all of these factors and has been shown to be an effective way to approach healthy eating.

The Mediterranean Diet

The Mediterranean diet is made up mostly of foods that are traditionally eaten in countries bordering the Mediterranean Sea. At least sixteen countries border the Mediterranean Sea, and cuisines vary from country to country. Traditional diets in countries such as Greece, Italy, Turkey, Israel, and Egypt, however, do have certain features in common: high consumption of fruits and vegetables

The Mediterranean diet is a low-cholesterol diet with a high consumption of fruits, vegetables, olives, breads, potatoes, and nuts and low consumption of red meats, dairy products, and wine.

and of other plant products such as breads, potatoes, nuts and seeds; use of olive oil instead of lard in cooking; low consumption of dairy products and red meat; and low to moderate consumption of wine. Studies show that a Mediterranean diet reduces a person's risk of both heart disease and cancer.

Dieticians think that a Mediterranean diet is good for the heart for several reasons. One is that saturated fat levels are kept low—more than half the calories in a Mediterranean diet typically come from unsaturated fats found in foods such as avocados, nuts, and olive oil. Another reason is that breads eaten in the Mediterranean region tend to be made from whole grains, which are higher in fiber, vitamins, and minerals than breads made from white flour. According to a study published on the *British Medical Journal* website in 2009, however, the most important aspect of the Mediterranean diet for health was the high consumption of fruits and vegetables. "Once again there is clear data that the healthiest foods grow in the ground,"[14] comments Mitchell Roslin, a surgeon at New York's Lenox Hill Hospital. "Mountains of evidence shows the more [fruits and vegetables], the better, period," agrees Keith-Thomas Ayoob, a nutritionist at the Albert Einstein College of Medicine. "They're loaded with fiber, antioxidants, and they're where you'll find a bucket of vitamins and minerals. The challenge is to eat them every day and preferably at least one at every meal."[15]

A few researchers, though, point out that the strength of the Mediterranean diet may be that it is low in sugar, processed foods, and saturated fats. "One of the strengths of the Mediterranean diet," says New York nutritionist Jana Klauer, "is what it does not contain: high amounts of sugar and preservatives. . . . The standard American diet stimulates the craving for sweet taste through overly sweetened foods."[16]

Reducing Cholesterol

Understanding the blood tests that doctors prescribe when they are trying to assess a patient's heart health is important for understanding how a diet low in saturated fat and high in soluble fiber can help prevent disease. Blood tests provide two important indicators of cardiovascular health: cholesterol levels and triglyceride levels. High levels of fat in the blood are associated with atherosclerosis, the buildup of plaque in the arteries. Both cholesterol and triglycerides are types of fat that tend to decrease in a person who eats a diet high in fruits and vegetables.

Cholesterol levels are complicated, though, because the blood contains both "good" cholesterol and "bad" cholesterol. LDL cholesterol is bad cholesterol—the kind that can

The Development of Atherosclerosis

Atherosclerosis is a disease in which plaque builds up inside your arteries. Arteries are blood vessels that carry oxygen-rich blood to your heart and parts of your body.

Plaque is made up of fat, cholesterol, calcium, and other substances found in the blood. Over time, plaque hardens and narrows your arteries, limiting the flow of oxygen-rich blood to your organs and other parts of your body. This can lead to serious problems, including heart attack, stroke, or even death.

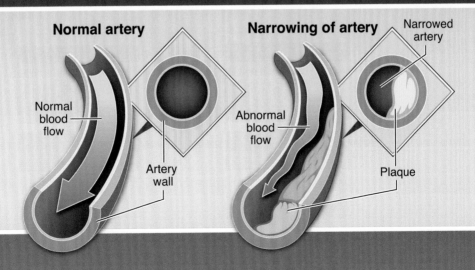

Taken from: www.nhlbi.nih.gov/health/dci/Diseases/Atherosclerosis/Atherosclerosis_WhatIs.html.

be deposited in the arteries. LDL cholesterol increases the chances that a person will develop atherosclerosis, or that the artery walls will become thick and hard. HDL cholesterol, on the other hand, is good cholesterol. HDL cholesterol carries cholesterol to the liver, where it can be processed so the body can excrete it.

Nutritionists now know that the different kinds of fat in the diet affect the body's cholesterol levels in different ways. Overall, fat should make up between 20 and 35 percent of the diet. To keep the heart healthy, the diet should be higher in healthy, good fats, like the fats that can be found in vegetables, and lower in unhealthy, bad fats, like the fat that can be found in meat and dairy products. Saturated fats (bad fats) tend to increase LDL cholesterol and clog the arteries, while the unsaturated fats (good fats) in olive oil and nuts have the opposite effect. Unsaturated fats increase HDL cholesterol and seem to help the blood to flow more freely through veins and arteries.

NUTRITION FACT

HDL and LDL mean high-density and low-density lipoprotein. The body uses lipoproteins to carry fat between tissues.

To reduce cholesterol levels, the diet should also include plenty of soluble fiber. Fiber can reduce the amount of LDL cholesterol in the blood. Soluble fiber can attach itself to cholesterol in the intestines, helping to carry cholesterol out of the body and preventing it from being absorbed into the bloodstream. Studies show that for every one or two grams of soluble fiber that people ingest, LDL cholesterol drops by another percentage point. According to the American Heart Association, a healthy diet should include foods that are high in soluble fiber, such as oatmeal and oat bran, beans, barley, citrus fruits, strawberries, and apples.

Researchers are beginning to find out that keeping LDL cholesterol low may do more than protect against heart disease and stroke. It may also protect against certain kinds of cancer, especially prostate cancer. Preliminary research shows that prostate cancer tumors grow faster when LDL cholesterol levels in the blood are higher.

What Are Trans Fats?

During the twentieth century, food manufacturers, looking for a fat that would not spoil during transportation and that would not break apart when heated repeatedly in restaurants, began to use partially hydrogenated fats in their foods. Partially hydrogenated fats are made by forcing hydrogen gas to bubble through vegetable oil. Commercial food manufacturers relied on partially hydrogenated fats for years. They told consumers that products made with partially hydrogenated fats were healthier because they contained vegetable oils, not saturated animal fats such as lard.

Late in the twentieth century, however, researchers determined that partially hydrogenated oils are not any healthier than saturated fats. In fact, these fats, which today are called trans fats, are even worse for the arteries than saturated fats. Doctors and scientists now believe that eliminating trans fats from the US food supply could prevent as many as one out of every five heart attacks and resulting deaths. Trans fats have not been banned, but food manufacturers must now add trans fats to their labels if a food contains more than one gram of trans fat per serving.

These unhealthy foods contain hydrogenated vegetable oil, or trans fats. Though not banned, food manufacturers must let the consumer know how much trans fats are in their products.

Reducing the Risk of Diabetes

A diet that is rich in fruits and vegetables and limits meat and dairy products does more than reduce cholesterol in the blood—it also helps to keep blood sugar levels stable. High blood sugar levels can lead to the development of type 2 diabetes. High blood sugar levels are also associated with heart disease, because glucose contains chemicals that inhibit the relaxation of blood vessels. This can make a person more likely to develop high blood pressure and narrowing of the arteries. "We know diabetes is a major risk factor for cardiovascular disease and we think this is one of the reasons,"[17] says Rita Tostes, a physiologist at the Medical College of Georgia School of Medicine.

About 57 million Americans have blood sugar levels that are high enough to classify these people as having prediabetes, which means they are at very high risk for developing type 2 diabetes. The good news is that prediabetes can be reversed. The Diabetes Prevention Program, a major study of prediabetics in the United States, published findings in 2002 in the *New England Journal of Medicine* showing that a healthy diet and exercise reduced each prediabetic's risk of becoming diabetic by 58 percent over a three-year period. In addition, once a person becomes diabetic, a healthy diet and exercise can reduce his or her risk of heart disease and stroke by up to 50 percent.

The key to reducing the risk of becoming diabetic is keeping blood sugar levels stable and avoiding sudden spikes of high blood sugar. One reason fruits and vegetables help lower blood sugar is that they are high in fiber. Dietary fiber can help blood sugar levels to remain steady and even rather than go through sudden spikes and dips. Fiber slows down digestion, so sugar from food is released into the bloodstream at a slower, more even pace. Meals that are high in refined carbohydrates, such as white bread and pasta, on the other hand, produce sudden blood sugar spikes, because the body absorbs this sugar more quickly.

Another way to reduce blood glucose levels is to reduce the amount of processed sugar in the diet. In a 2009 study published in the *Archives of Pediatric and Adolescent Medi-*

cine, one group of teens was asked to reduce sugar intake by the equivalent of one can of soda per day, and another group was asked to increase fiber by an amount equivalent to half a cup of beans per day. Researchers studied Latino teens, who are at especially high risk for type 2 diabetes. The study showed that reducing sugar caused the pancreas to release 33 percent less insulin—making it less likely that the teens would develop insulin resistance and become prediabetic or diabetic. Those who increased their fiber intake averaged a 10 percent reduction in abdominal fat, thereby lowering their risk of developing insulin resistance.

Eliminating soda from the diet, or simply reducing it as the teens in the 2009 study did, is a good first step for prediabetics who do not want to become diabetic. Several studies have linked the high-fructose corn syrup in soda with the development of type 2 diabetes, especially in children and teens. In addition, high-fructose corn syrup is associated with high blood pressure, so eliminating it from the diet may also reduce a person's risk of heart disease.

NUTRITION FACT

13 Percent

Almost 13 percent of American adults have diabetes.

Fruit also contains sugar that can raise blood glucose levels, so nutritionists discourage kids from drinking large amounts of fruit juice. Fruit itself, on the other hand, can be part of a healthy diet for most people. The one major difference between the sugar in a piece of fruit and the sugar in fruit juice, corn syrup, or table sugar is that the sugar in fruit is digested slowly because it is combined with fiber—the other sugars are not. Table sugar, corn syrup, and the sugar in fruit juice are combined with nothing that will slow down their absorption or regulate blood glucose levels. Instead, they enter the bloodstream quickly, causing blood sugar levels, and shortly thereafter, blood insulin levels, to spike. Even if the body does not develop insulin resistance as a result of ingesting so much sugar, it will store unused sugar as fat. In the long term, this trend can produce obesity. In the short term, a sugar spike may be followed by a sugar slump, causing feelings of fatigue, low energy, and depression.

Avoiding Carcinogens

Not only do fruits and vegetables help keep blood sugar levels steady, but they are low in carcinogens. A carcinogen is a substance or exposure that can lead to cancer. Not everyone who is exposed to a carcinogen develops cancer, but the greater the amount of the exposure, the more likely it is that the person will develop cancer as a result.

Fast food restaurant grilled chicken often contains PhIP, a carcinogen that increases the risk of prostate, colon, rectum, and breast cancers.

Most recently, scientists have found carcinogens in cooked meats and several other cooked foods. A 2008 study conducted by lead researcher Kristie Sullivan and published in *Nutrition and Cancer*, for example, found that grilled chicken from fast food restaurants usually contains PhIP, a powerful carcinogen that increases the risk of cancers of the prostate, colon, rectum, and breast. In fact, any food that is cooked to the point of browning or burning, including whole-grain toast, contains another carcinogen: polycyclic aromatic hydrocarbons, or PAHs. These are the same carcinogens that are found in soot and in burned wood. PAHs increase the risk of colon cancer for those who ingest them, and they also increase the risk of lung cancer for cooks who breathe in PAH particles.

Scientists have engaged in years of research to establish what substances are carcinogenic and also to determine what substances help to prevent cancer. Research shows that eating a diet low in calories, low in animal fat and meat, and high in fruits, vegetables, and whole grains will reduce a person's risk of the most common cancers. Fresh fruits and vegetables are so helpful in preventing cancer that some researchers consider them to be anticarcinogens.

Phytochemicals

Fruits and vegetables help to prevent cancer in three ways. First, they are rich in vitamins and minerals, which nourish the body in general, better preparing the body to defend itself against disease. Second, they are high in fiber, which helps to carry toxins out of the body.

The third and most important reason that fruits and vegetables can help prevent cancer is that they are rich in phytochemicals. Phytochemicals are substances that can affect living tissue in the body. Thousands of phytochemicals have been found in fruits and vegetables. These chemicals are what give plants their unique flavor, color, texture, and odor. For example, garlic's sulfurous smell comes from the phytochemical allicin. Many phytochemicals block the formation of cancer tumors. Others cause cells to reproduce themselves less often, giving the cells fewer opportunities to mutate. Some reduce the production of estrogen in the body, making the body less susceptible to hormone-related cancers such as breast cancer. Many phytochemicals also reduce a person's risk of heart disease and stroke by lowering cholesterol and blood pressure, reducing blood clot formation, and reducing damage to blood vessel walls.

The most common cancer to be caused by an inadequate diet is colorectal cancer—cancer of the colon or rectum—the last section of the large intestine that waste passes through before it exits the body. One of the primary causes of colorectal cancer is eating too much red meat and not enough fruits and vegetables. Obesity, drinking an excessive amount of alcohol, and lack of exercise are also thought to be triggers for the development of cancer in the colon and/or rectum. The same factors can also cause prostate cancer in men. Many other cancers can also be prevented with a healthy diet. According to the American Cancer Society, about one-third of the cancers that resulted in deaths in 2009 could be attributed to obesity, lack of exercise, and malnutrition.

Maintaining a Healthy Weight

In addition to eating a healthy diet, one of the most important factors in preventing disease is maintaining a healthy weight. Staying at a healthy weight by eating right can help prevent heart disease, stroke, cancer, and diabetes. For example, eating right and maintaining a healthy weight can help people keep their blood sugar in check, which can help prevent diabetes. A 2009 Loyola University study showed that more than 60 percent of diabetic adults are obese, and 21 percent end up becoming morbidly obese—100 pounds (45.4kg) or more overweight.

People who are overweight or obese are at risk for numerous other health problems, as the National Heart, Lung, and Blood Institute explains: "Being overweight is a risk factor for health problems such as diabetes, high blood pressure, high cholesterol and triglycerides, arthritis, gall bladder disease, gynecologic problems, some cancers, and even lung

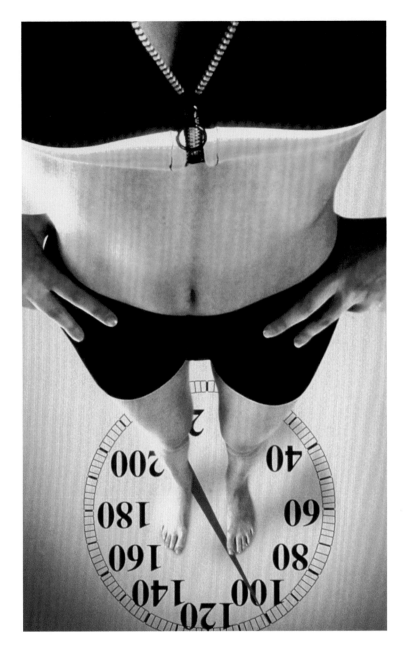

problems."[18] Losing excess weight and staying at a healthy weight, on the other hand, will help a person feel more fit and energetic, as well as help lower a person's risk for weight-related health problems. One of the most important ways in which maintaining a healthy weight helps to prevent disease is by reducing inflammation.

Reducing Inflammation

Losing weight causes an overweight or obese person's chances of having a heart attack to drop dramatically because it helps lower chemicals in the body that cause inflammation. This was borne out by a 2008 study conducted by heart specialists at Johns Hopkins University and published in the *Journal of the American College of Cardiology*. "The biological effects of obesity on the heart are quite profound," remarks Joao Lima of Johns Hopkins University, commenting on a 2008 study. "Even if obese people feel otherwise healthy, there are measurable and early chemical signs of damage to their heart."[19] Lima was referring to chemicals that researchers found in the blood of obese people who later developed heart failure. These chemicals (interleukin-6, C-reactive protein, and fibrinogen) are produced naturally by the body in response to disease. They cause inflammation—redness, localized warmth or fever, and swelling. Normally, inflammation is part of the body's healing process. Problems arise when inflammation occurs repeatedly in the same area (such as the heart), because it can damage cells and cause scar tissue to build up. In addition to increasing a person's chances of developing heart disease, chronic inflammation all over the body also increases the risk of developing cancer and type 2 diabetes.

Researchers are not sure why inflammatory chemicals tend to build up in the blood of people who are obese. Some scientists think that atherosclerosis may be connected with a chronic low-grade infection of the blood vessels. Atherosclerosis is the process by which the walls of the arteries become thick with plaque, leaving less room for blood to pass through.

Even though scientists are not certain why overweight and obese people have more inflammation, they are certain that eating more fruits and vegetables can help not only with maintaining a healthy weight but also with lowering

Broccoli Sprouts Protect Airways

Dieticians have been encouraging people to eat broccoli for years, since broccoli is a good source of many vitamins and minerals and is rich in fiber. In 2009 a University of California at Los Angeles study showed that broccoli provides additional health benefits. Broccoli and other cruciferous vegetables such as cabbage, kale, and cauliflower contain a substance that protects human airways from inflammation. Airways can become inflamed in response to asthma, allergies, chronic lung diseases, and bacterial or viral infections such as the ones that cause colds, flu, and pneumonia.

In the study, researchers worked with a group of sixty-five volunteers. One set of volunteers was given broccoli sprouts to eat every day, while the other set ate alfalfa sprouts daily. (Alfalfa sprouts do not contain the substance that researchers believe protects human airways.) The volunteers who ate broccoli sprouts were two to three times less likely to develop inflamed airways than the volunteers who had only alfalfa sprouts. "This strategy," says Marc Reidl, the primary author of the study, "could lead to potential treatments for a variety of respiratory conditions." It is too early for researchers to recommend that people eat a particular amount of broccoli or other cruciferous vegetables every day. Right now they are only recommending that people include these vegetables in their diets regularly.

ScienceDaily, "Broccoli May Help Protect Against Respiratory Conditions like Asthma," March 4, 2009. www .sciencedaily.com/releases/2009/03/090302133218.htm.

Cruciferous vegetables like cauliflower, cabbage, brussels sprouts, and broccoli are good sources of vitamins C and B and protect the human lungs from inflammation.

inflammation. Many of the phytochemicals found in fruits and vegetables are antioxidants, chemicals that reduce inflammation in the body. "People who are obese need more fruits, vegetables, legumes, and wholesome unrefined grains," says Heather Vincent, a professor at the University of Florida's Orthopedics and Sports Medicine Institute. "In comparison to a normal-weight person, an obese person is always going to be behind the eight ball because there are so many adverse metabolic processes going on."[20]

Antioxidants, though, are good for everyone, not just people who are overweight or obese. "Inflammation is now considered to be a central part of all chronic diseases, including aging," says Paul Talalay of the Johns Hopkins Medical School. "The same pathological processes are involved in aging as in skin cancer and neurodegenerative diseases."[21] The antioxidants in fruits and vegetables have also been found to reduce the inflammation of acne, arthritis, respiratory diseases, and even age-related wrinkling.

A Rainbow on a Plate

Eating a wide variety of fruits and vegetables is a good way to ensure the diet contains the nutrients the body needs. Nutritionists say that the best way to consume more fruits and vegetables is to think in terms of color—the more different colors appear on a person's plate, the better for his or her health. "Lots of variety means the nutrients can act in synergy [combined effort] for a powerful effect,"[22] says dietician Andrea Dunn, who works at the Cleveland Clinic. For example, in the course of a day, a person might have red tomatoes, white garlic, blueberries or purple grapes, oranges, and dark green lettuce or zucchini. One way to include a lot of variety is to eat green salad or fruit salad with lots of different ingredients. Another option is to add a rainbow of vegetables to pasta and sauce, to salsa, to stir-fries, or to stews and soups.

"One thing people can do," says nutrition professor Penny Kris-Etherton of Penn State University, "is incorporate more fruits and vegetables into foods they normally eat."[23] Kris-

Etherton suggests adding a single-serving carton of apple-sauce and half a banana to a bowl of oatmeal in the morning. She likes to put roasted red peppers and asparagus spears on her turkey sandwiches. She also recommends substituting vegetables for some of the meat in recipes—replacing some of the ground beef in spaghetti sauce with chopped red bell peppers, for example.

Taking the rainbow approach to fruits and vegetables ensures a diet with a variety of nutrients.

Another way to fit more fruits and vegetables into the diet is to use the approach recommended by the Harvard School of Public Health. Harvard's nutritionists tell people to think in terms of a plateful of food. At each meal, half of the plate should be covered with fruit or vegetables. The fruits and vegetables on that half of the plate should be as colorful as possible.

Eating a diet based on a wide variety of fruits and vegetables and low in meat, dairy products, and saturated fat is widely viewed by nutritionists as the best choice for human health. Fruits and vegetables are high in phytochemicals, antioxidants, vitamins, minerals, and fiber. They are also low in calories and fat. By regulating the levels of cholesterol and glucose in the blood, as well as reducing inflammation all over the body, a diet based on fruits and vegetables dramatically reduces a person's risk of obesity, cardiovascular disease, cancer, and diabetes.

CHAPTER **4**

What Governments and Organizations Are Doing

I n the United States and in most other industrialized countries, government agencies and nonprofit organizations collect data and distribute information about diet and disease. By doing studies and making policy changes, governments and organizations respond to growing levels of disease around the world. A main focus is the growing rate of obesity, which is of particular concern because obesity contributes to so many diseases that are highly preventable. Also of concern is malnutrition, which contributes to diseases and deaths around the world. Other major areas of concern include heart disease, liver disease, diabetes, and metabolic syndrome. Government and private organizations alike are taking action to help people make choices about nutrition and their diet that will help in the battle to prevent disease.

Collecting and Distributing Data

In the United States, the primary agencies that are responsible for collecting and distributing information about diet and disease are the US Food and Drug Administration, the Centers for Disease Control and Prevention, and the National Institutes of Health. These organizations are the parents of many other smaller agencies, such as the

The USDA first began to distribute the food pyramid chart of nutrition information in 1992. It replaced the earlier Food Wheel version developed in the '70s.

National Cancer Institute and the National Center for Health Statistics. In addition, the US Department of Agriculture (USDA) collects supplemental information regarding nutrition. The information gathered by the USDA was originally used to create the four food groups chart that was used to teach children about nutrition in the 1970s and 1980s. Today information gathered by the USDA is used to prepare the food pyramid, which also provides dietary guidelines.

In addition to the statistics that are collected by government agencies, doctors and nutritionists who want to get a big picture of the trends in diet and disease can turn to nonprofit organizations that also collect statistics. In the United States, the National Academy of Sciences and the Institute of Medicine are two such organizations. Many others focus on particular issues or diseases: the American Heart Association, the American Stroke Association, the American Cancer Society, and the American Diabetes Association.

Similar organizations exist internationally. Two of the most prominent are part of the United Nations: the World Health Organization and the United Nations Children's Fund. These organizations try to provide information and assistance to people who have diseases, while also supporting research that enables doctors to learn more.

A Call to Arms

Once government agencies and nonprofit organizations collect statistics that show a worrying health trend—such as an increase in a certain type of disease or a tendency for people to develop a combination of certain diseases—doctors, scientists, and policy makers in the government respond to it. Doctors watch for signs of the new trend in their patients, scientists conduct studies to try to learn more, and policy makers advocate new laws in an attempt to create healthier trends. One example of the way this process works can be seen in the rise of and response to metabolic syndrome.

During the past twenty years, doctors began to notice a startling new trend—an increase in the numbers of children and teens developing heart disease. Doctors used to assume that young people were too young to have to worry about heart disease—heart disease was thought to be a health risk for older and middle-aged Americans, not kids. Today, though, according to a 2008 American Heart Association study, many obese children and teens have arteries similar to those of the average forty-five-year-old. About 9 percent of US teenagers, including some teenagers who are overweight but not obese, have metabolic syndrome. Of obese teenagers, more than one-quarter have metabolic syndrome.

Metabolic syndrome, which is common in adults, is a condition in which the same person has multiple risk factors for both heart disease and type 2 diabetes. Sometimes called syndrome X, metabolic syndrome is defined as having at least three of the following risk factors: too much fat around the waist, high blood pressure, high blood sugar, high levels of fat in the blood, and abnormal cholesterol levels. People with metabolic syndrome are at very high risk for developing heart disease, stroke, or type 2 diabetes.

Doctors say that metabolic syndrome is even starting to show up in very young kids. Most obese kids end up developing metabolic syndrome as adults if they do not have it as children or teens, and about 17 percent of American kids are obese by the age of eight. Many obese kids have developed serious heart problems by the time they are teenagers. When doctors began to see young children with metabolic syndrome, they were horrified. University of Miami researcher Sarah Messiah warns:

> If a kid is age eight with metabolic syndrome, it will take 10 years or less for that child to become a type 2 diabetic or develop heart disease. . . . So as these kids enter adulthood, they could be faced with an entire life of chronic disease. . . . It is sad because these children are so young and I don't know if they have ever really known what feeling good feels like.[24]

The development of metabolic syndrome in children became a call to arms, initially for the doctors and researchers who had been the first to learn about it, and eventually for parents, educators, and government policy makers. Writing in the June 2009 edition of the *American Journal of Medicine*, Joseph Alpert argues that if Americans do not start to make healthier lifestyle choices, chronic disease rates will only increase. He calls for government, school, and corporate action, writing: "The time is now long overdue to start aggressive preventive cardiovascular disease programs in our schools, our homes, and our worksites."[25]

Preventing Metabolic Syndrome

In 2006 the National Institutes of Health (NIH), a government agency that collects statistics and information related to health and medicine, decided to take action to help prevent metabolic syndrome. The NIH is part of the US Department of Health and Human Services. It is a federal government agency that conducts and supports medical research, making that research available to doctors, scientists, researchers, and the general public. The NIH called together a group of doctors, including pediatricians, cardiologists, endocrinolo-

People with metabolic syndrome have too much fat around the waist and have high blood pressure and high blood sugar levels.

gists, and other specialists to brainstorm ways to reduce the number of child cases of metabolic syndrome.

One of the first things that NIH specialists, as well as other specialists who became concerned about metabolic syndrome over the years, decided to do was to spread the word. In 2007 the International Diabetes Federation (IDF) introduced a new definition of metabolic syndrome, aimed at catching children who are at risk for type 2 diabetes, heart disease, and stroke as early as possible. The new definition allows pediatricians to diagnose children using abdominal circumference, blood pressure, and blood test results such as elevated triglycerides, low HDL (or good) cholesterol, and blood glucose levels.

At the same time, the IDF also called for governments around the world to do more to prevent metabolic syndrome. Professor George Alberti, a past president of IDF and coauthor of the new definition, explains:

> Early detection followed by treatment—particularly lifestyle intervention—is vital to halt the progression of the metabolic syndrome and safeguard the future health of children and adolescents. . . . We call on governments to create environments that allow for lifestyle changes. This will require a coordinated approach across all sectors including health, education, sports and agriculture, but it is the only way we can curb the burden of type 2 diabetes and cardiovascular disease.[26]

Scientists and researchers also resolved to study metabolic syndrome further. Metabolic syndrome is still so new—as are pediatric variations of heart disease, atherosclerosis, and type 2 diabetes—that researchers decided they needed to know more about how these conditions develop in children and teens. Better information, they felt, could be used later, not only by doctors advising patients but by legislators and by government regulatory agencies trying to set policies related to school lunches and health insurance.

Knowing that preventing a disease is easier than reversing it, researchers first tried studying populations of obese children and teens, trying to determine what factors, such as weight or diet, might cause one child to develop heart disease or diabetes while another equally obese child did not develop those diseases. Researchers at Yale University followed a group of sixty obese teens for three years beginning in 2005, checking their glucose levels

NUTRITION FACT

71 Percent

Given the choice, children will choose to drink soda, rather than water or milk, 71 percent of the time, according to a 2006 poll.

at periodic intervals. During the study period 23 percent of the teens became gradually more resistant to insulin. "There are differences in the prediabetes forms, already in children," mused Yale professor of pediatrics Sonia Caprio. "There is an evolution that gradually takes place. They go from normal glucose tolerance to impaired glucose tolerance, and there are two defects, both insulin resistance and early defects in pancreatic . . . function," she continued. Caprio did not know why some children began the progression toward diabetes and others did not, but vowed to continue her research. "We need to understand why they already have the predisposition to prediabetes," she said, "and how we can reverse or prevent it."[27]

Liver Disease

The same group of insulin-resistant teens studied at Yale began to deposit more fat in their liver and muscles at the same time that they were becoming more insulin resistant. Seeing this, researchers began to see a connection that helped explain the spike in the number of children and teenagers who need liver transplants. Liver disease used to be primarily a disease of alcoholism. The liver is the body organ that is responsible for filtering toxins—such as alcohol—out of the blood. When adults die of liver failure after a lifetime of alcohol abuse, people often say that they "drank themselves to death." What they mean is that alcoholics drink to excess so many times that their livers finally give out.

The liver does more than just filter toxins out of the blood. It also helps the body to digest fat. As more and more Americans become obese, doctors are seeing a rise in nonalcoholic fatty liver disease (NAFLD). Doctors are finding many obese children and teens (their average age is fourteen) who have NAFLD.

"This dwarfs diabetes in terms of prevalence," says pediatrician Jeffrey Schwimmer of the University of California at San Diego's Department of Pediatrics. "There's no question that this is the most chronic, serious consequence of childhood obesity. It deserves way more attention. The majority of children who have NAFLD are undiagnosed."[28] Studies show that nearly 10 percent of US children between the ages of two and nineteen have NAFLD, which is hard to diagnose because it does not produce any symptoms. Many will develop cirrhosis of the liver as a result of NAFLD. Cirrhosis is a condition in which the liver is repeatedly damaged and scar tissue replaces much of the liver's healthy tissue. Eventually, the liver cannot function anymore. Cirrhosis can be fatal for a child who does not get a liver transplant.

Children and teens with NAFLD are more than thirteen times as likely as children who do not have this disorder to die within twenty years or to find themselves in need of a liver transplant. Receiving a liver transplant does not solve a person's health problems, either—people who have transplants must take immune system–suppressing drugs for the rest of their lives to prevent their bodies from attacking the unfamiliar liver.

Realizing that children were experiencing liver damage as well as cardiovascular damage and that they were also at risk for type 2 diabetes and certain kinds of cancer stiffened the resolve of children's health advocates. They began to call upon governments to take concrete action to prevent these diseases, such as providing nutrition information for consumers and improving the diets of schoolchildren.

Information Resources

One action health advocates requested of the government was to make nutrition information more easily available to the public. In 2004 the USDA launched a new website devoted to nutrition. The website is at www.nutrition.gov. It is designed to pull together nutrition information from several government agencies into one tool that can be accessed by the public. Former agriculture secretary Ann Veneman explained that members of the public needed access to reliable information about nutrition in order to make informed choices about diet. The new website includes specialized information about nutrition for men, women, and children of various ages.

Another action designed to provide nutrition information to the public was to change the labels that manufacturers are required to put on food packages. Nutrition

How to Read a Nutrition Label

Serving size: Serving sizes are listed in standard measurements, such as cups or pieces. Similar foods usually have similar serving sizes, so you can compare them more easily. The label also includes servings per container to help you calculate the calories and nutrients in the entire package. Be sure to check the serving size against how much you actually eat. If a serving is 16 crackers and you eat 32, that also doubles the calories, fat, and other nutrients you eat.

Calories: The calories listed is the number of calories in one serving of food. The label also shows how many calories come from fat. In this example, 50 of the 150 calories come from fat. You can use this information to compare similar products and choose the one that is lower in either calories or fat, or both calories and fat.

Nutrients: At a minimum, the product must list the amounts of total fat, saturated fat, trans fat, cholesterol, sodium, total carbohydrates, dietary fiber, sugars, protein, Vitamins A and C, calcium and iron that are in one serving. This can help you track whether you're getting all the nutrients you need in a day—or too much.

Nutrition Facts

Serving Size 1 cup (31 g)
Serving Per Container 9

Amount Per Serving

Calories 150	Calories from Fat 50

	% Daily Values*
Total Fat 12 g	**9%**
Saturated Fat 1 g	**6%**
Trans Fat 1 g	
Polyunsaturated Fat 1 g	
Monunsaturated Fat 1 g	
Cholesterol 0 mg	**10%**
Sodium 270 mg	**20%**
Total Carbohydrates 21 g	**7%**
Dietary Fiber 1 g	**4%**
Sugars 3 g	
Protein 5 g	

Vitamin A	4%
Vitamin C	2%
Calcium	20%
Iron	4%

*Percent Daily Values are passed on a 2,000 calorie diet. Your Daily Values may be higher or lower depending on your calorie needs.

		Calories	2,000	2,500
Total Fat	Less than		65 g	80 g
Sat Fat	Less than		20 g	25 g
Cholesterol	Less than		300 mg	300 mg
Sodium	Less than		2,400 mg	2,400 mg
Total Carbohydrates			300 g	375 g
Dietary Fiber			25 g	30 g

Footnote: The footnote at the bottom of the label is a reminder that the Percent Daily Value is based on a 2,000-calorie-a-day diet. The footnote contains a statement saying that nutrient values vary by a person's particular calorie needs. If there is enough space on the product package, the footnote includes a list of selected nutrient values for both 2,000 and 2,500-calorie-a-day diets. Keep in mind that many people, including women and older adults or those trying to lose weight may need fewer than 2,000 calories, while other may need 2,500 calories or more. So think of 2,000-calories-a-day as a general reference point.

Taken from: Food and Drug Administration, 2006.

information has been included on food packages for many years, but Congress periodically passes laws changing the requirements. Food manufacturers are required to list a food's ingredients on the label. In addition, Congress passed a law in 2004 requiring labels to list any major food allergens (milk, eggs, fish, crustacean shellfish, tree nuts, wheat, peanuts, or soybeans) that are included in a food. The nutrition facts on a food's label must include total calories per serving and the amount of fat, protein, fiber, and carbohydrates in a food. Packages also list the percentage of the recommended daily allowance of various vitamins and minerals that a food contains.

In 2009 Congress passed a law allowing some foods to have a green checkmark as part of their packaging. Foods with a green checkmark are classified as a "smart choice." To receive the checkmark, foods have to limit fat, cholesterol, sodium, and added sugars. The foods also have to include a certain amount of at least one of the following nutrients: calcium, potassium, fiber, magnesium, vitamin A, vitamin C, or vitamin E. Texas A&M professor of nutrition Joanne Lupton explains, "You will be able to walk into a supermarket and know . . . that a product with a checkmark is better for you than a product without a checkmark."[29]

Healthier School Lunches

Unquestionably, obesity is closely related to the development of several highly preventable diseases. Many critics have pointed a finger at school lunches as a major cause for overweight and obesity among American teens. Michael Schloss, a heart disease prevention specialist at New York University, is one such critic. "If you've seen what's on the menu for most school lunches, these findings are no surprise,"[30] he commented, reacting to a study showing an increase in heart disease and metabolic syndrome among teenagers.

Since 2005 many state legislatures have passed laws revising their nutrition standards for school lunches and for foods that are dispensed in school vending machines. In 2005 forty-two state legislatures passed new laws regarding food that is served to children and teens in school. "This

Bring Healthy Food Back

Activists such as chef Ann Cooper have been advocating a change in school lunches for many years. Cooper has developed an idea for bringing healthy food back to school cafeterias: the Lunch Box project. The idea is for schools to provide whole foods that are bought locally and prepared from scratch for students. Cooper and others are hopeful that her idea will catch on. One sign that they are meeting with success came in 2009 when Cooper was invited to a conference of the School Nutrition Association to discuss her Lunch Box project. Says Cooper, "All of a sudden I am not the fringe idiot trying to get everyone to serve peas and carrots that don't come out of a can, like that's the most radical idea they have ever heard of."[1] Supporters of Cooper's project include Senator Kirsten Gillibrand of New York, who commented, "If you feed a kid chicken nuggets and canned peas and Doritos and canned fruit as a school lunch or you feed him grilled chicken, steamed broccoli and fresh fruits and a whole grain roll, the difference is night and day."[2]

1. Quoted in Kim Severson, "Stars Aligning on School Lunches," *New York Times,* August 18, 2009. www.nytimes.com/2009/08/19/dining/19school.html.
2. Quoted in Severson, "Stars Aligning on School Lunches."

has been a watershed year for state legislation dealing with school nutrition," says Amy Winterfeld, a National Conference of State Legislatures health policy analyst. "There has been a wide range of legislation covering everything from offering healthier beverages to eliminating deep fat frying."[31]

Some legislators want to pull vending machines out of schools altogether. "One of our top priorities," says Margo Wootan, nutrition policy director at the Center for Science in the Public Interest, "is to get soda and junk food out of school."[32] That goal has proved difficult to accomplish. In many schools, the money from vending machine sales is used to provide funding for the school lunch program. School boards fear that they will be unable to pay for the school lunch program if they get rid of the vending machines. In 2005 vending machines could be found in 98 percent of high schools, 97 percent of middle/junior high schools, and 27 percent of elementary schools.

National school lunch legislation has existed since 1946, when Congress first passed the National School Lunch Act. At the time, it was intended partially to nourish children and partially to ensure a market for crops produced by American farmers. The lunch program was expanded with the passage of the Child Nutrition Act in 1966, when a milk program and a breakfast program were added. In 2010 President Barack Obama proposed a $1 billion increase for the Child Nutrition Act, prompting a national discussion of childhood obesity and nutrition. Despite reforms in state school lunch legislation in a majority of states, most states still allow junk food to be sold on campuses. California is one of the rare states to limit sugar and fat in student meals.

A Marketing Opportunity

While government agencies and nonprofit organizations have responded to growing levels of disease by doing studies and making policy changes, some corporations have also taken action. In 2003, while several state legislatures pondered whether to require restaurants to provide nutrition labels on menus, several restaurant chains added nutrition calculators to their websites. Many fast food restaurants have added salad bars and fruit side dishes. According to Neil Stern, an advertising consultant for the fast food industry, though, consumers were not convinced by restaurants' ad campaigns. Stern noted that the only fast food restaurant that successfully convinced consumers it served healthy food was Subway. "Subway makes people feel good about what they are eating," he said, but he added that since most Subway customers do not buy low-fat meals, "more or less they're buying a fantasy."[33]

The legislatures that were considering forcing restaurants to add nutrition labeling to their menus wound up not doing so. In spite of this, in 2008 Yum! Brands, the parent company of Taco Bell, KFC, A&W Restaurants, Pizza Hut, and Long John Silver's, announced that it would start adding nutrition information to its menu boards.

Not everyone pays attention to nutrition information provided by corporations, but some people do. Brothers Scott and Chris Mocarski, of Tinley Park, Illinois, decided they wanted to try the Wendy's Baconator when it came out. "We knew it had to be so bad for you," remembers Chris. "We went online and found out it has, like, 3000 calories. So I went back to my spicy chicken sandwich."[34] The recommended daily intake of calories for an adult is 2,000 calories, so the Baconator was well over this amount.

Beginning in 2003 many fast food corporations started offering fruit bowls and salad bars in an effort to upgrade the nutritional value of their menus.

Improving Nutrition Worldwide

While American consumers debate over which sandwich to buy from a fast food restaurant, children and teens in many developing countries are still dying of diseases that are either caused by or made much worse by a lack of calories and protein. The United Nations contains several agencies that collect information and formulate policies that are intended to provide more nutritious food and help people around the world battle hunger and malnutrition. One of the leading agencies to fight starvation worldwide is the United Nations Food and Agriculture Organization (FAO). The FAO fights starvation by helping to provide tools and seeds for farmers in developing nations and by finding solutions to problems that arise in agriculture, fishing, and forestry. The FAO also fights against poverty by helping farmers and fishers make good marketing decisions. For example, in Bangladesh in October 2003, the FAO set up a thrice-weekly radio broadcast that would tell people what prices were being charged at different markets for cereals, grains, vegetables, spices, and fish. Farmers used that information to take whatever food they produced to a market where that food was in shorter supply, so they could charge more and earn a better living. At the same time, they were helping to reduce starvation by bringing food to where it was needed.

The United Nations is not the only world organization to address problems of hunger and malnutrition internationally. Other international organizations such as WHEAT (World Hunger Education, Advocacy, and Training) and the World Hunger Education Service focus on educating the public in industrial countries about hunger and malnutrition in the developing world. In addition, several religious organizations have made it their mission to feed the world's poor. These organizations include Baptist World Aid, Catholic Charities, the Church World Service (which bands several religious groups together to help the poor), Episcopal Relief and Development, Food for the Hungry, Living Waters for the World (a Presbyterian group),

No More Soda for Sale

After years of fighting with health advocates to keep soda in the vending machines in public schools, soft drink giants Coca-Cola, PepsiCo, Cadbury Schweppes, and several other beverage companies agreed to slowly replace the soda and other sugary drinks in school vending machines. The companies were working with the American Heart Association and the William J. Clinton Foundation. "This is really the beginning of a major effort to modify childhood obesity at the level of the school systems," noted Robert Eckel, the American Heart Association president.

In September 2006 the beverage companies signed the deal, agreeing to sell only 100 percent juice, low-fat milk, and bottled water in vending machines that are located on elementary and middle/junior high school grounds. In high schools vending machine choices are also limited but can include diet soda, sports drinks, tea, and flavored water. Nearly 35 million students attend the schools that were affected by the change.

Quoted in Lloyd de Vries, "Deal Halts Soda Sales in Schools," CBS News, May 3, 2006. www.cbsnews.com/stories/2006/05/03/health/main1582852.shtml.

As a result of the efforts of the William J. Clinton Foundation and others, school vending machines now have healthier snacks, bottled water, fruit juice, and sugar-free soft drinks.

Lutheran World Relief, MAZON: A Jewish Response to Hunger, the Mennonite Central Committee, the Muslims Against Hunger Project, and the United Methodist Committee on Relief.

Gradually, people in industrialized countries are becoming more educated about nutrition. Health advocates hope that they will apply that knowledge not only to improving nutrition in their own countries but to making sure that enough healthy food is provided for all the world's people.

CHAPTER 5

Teens Making a Difference Through Diet

Eighteen-year-old Amanda Nuñez knew why most of her friends did not like to eat vegetables. They wanted to eat food that tasted good. Vegetables are often boiled and baked until they turn into tasteless mush. "But there are ways to do it," Amanda says, so that vegetables will taste "better than chocolate cake."[35]

Amanda developed her own recipes for a heart-healthy Valentine's Day dinner. She came up with a recipe for vegetable pasta, including zucchini, grape or cherry tomatoes, asparagus, broccoli, garlic, olive oil, Parmesan cheese, and rigatoni. Dessert was "love berries," seasonal berries mixed with a lightly sweetened sauce. Then she submitted her work to the Art Institute's Best Teen Chef Competition—and won. She became the Best Teen Chef for 2007 and received a full tuition scholarship to attend the International Culinary School at the Art Institute of California–San Diego. While attending college and learning to be a chef, she is also learning on the job about healthy cooking by working at San Diego's Cin Cin Restaurant. Cin Cin specializes in providing healthy meals.

Making Healthier Choices

Following a healthy diet to help prevent disease is important even for teens, because diseases such as heart disease, type

2 diabetes, and even stroke are not limited to older people. This is a matter of great concern to health experts, who say teenagers eat a worse diet than the average American adult.

Since 1980 the number of American teenagers who are overweight has tripled. About 20 percent of American teens have cholesterol levels that put them at risk for developing heart disease. About 7 percent of teenagers are prediabetic—which means that they will probably become diabetic within ten years if they do not lose weight. Researchers expect that number to rise soon. For teenagers to have high blood pressure, high cholesterol levels, or to develop insulin resistance is not unusual. "With their overreliance on fat- and sugar-laden processed foods and a diet deficient in nutrient-rich fruits and vegetables, many American teenagers are walking time bombs for ill health,"[36] writes *New York Times* health columnist Jane Brody.

Many teenagers have begun to make healthier choices when it comes to what they eat. Those who study nutrition can be successful in changing their diets, especially if they are

Since 1980 the number of overweight American teenagers has tripled.

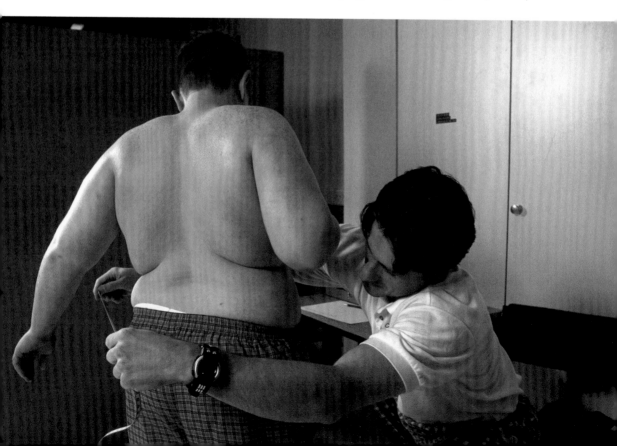

given support from their families and communities. Teens who participate in research studies on nutrition, for example, tend to maintain their diet changes even after the study is over. In one study of African American teenagers published in the journal *Hypertension* in August 1999, researchers tried adding high-potassium foods to teens' diets for three weeks to see if it would lower their blood pressure. Dawn Wilson of Virginia Commonwealth University, who was one of the authors of the study, commented: "We focused on dietary potassium, because, realistically, teenagers are more likely to add bananas, apples, baked potatoes or beef stew to their diet than give up high-salt, processed foods. . . . So we were doubling their intake daily. . . . They had fun doing it and they were allowed to make the decisions."[37] Not only did the added potassium work well to lower teens' blood pressure, but teenagers kept the changes in their diets for as long as two years after the study had concluded.

NUTRITION FACT
22 Percent
In 2009 about 22 percent of American young adults (aged sixteen to twenty-four) volunteered to help those less fortunate than themselves.

Healthy Choices in College

Recent studies also show that college students are applying what they learn about nutrition. Some students have had their awareness about nutrition raised in high school. Others have taken college classes on nutrition. Many universities now offer a nutrition class to incoming freshmen as part of their orientation. Partly as a result of this education on the link between diet and disease, in 2006 soda sales began to drop on college campuses for the first time in twenty years. Many students have begun to drink tea, such as green tea or black tea, instead of soda, energy drinks, or coffee.

"A quick caffeine fix that isn't unhealthy is diet sodas, but they really aren't good for you either," warned Samantha Muster, a human nutrition and food major at West Virginia University. "Even though they are calorie-free, the

Kids Cook 4 a Cause

Award-winning chef Rozanne Gold, a strong believer in teaching kids to cook, was putting together a new cookbook. Her book was called *Eat Fresh Food: Awesome Recipes for Teen Chefs,* and she needed teen chefs to test her recipes. One of those teen chefs was sixteen-year-old Ian Kimmel of Linwood, New Jersey.

Kimmel was fascinated by his experience cooking with Gold. He became so convinced of the importance of eating fruits and vegetables that he decided to form his own organization, Kids Cook 4 a Cause. Kimmel's organization provides classes that teach kids to cook. So far he has taught hundreds of kids between the ages of nine and seventeen to cook. Kimmel donates all of his profits to children's charities.

Another of Gold's teenage chefs was fifteen-year-old Danielle Hartog of Westport, Connecticut. Hartog lost 23 pounds (10.4kg) in seven months using recipes she learned from Gold. She commented later: "Once I started eating healthy and feeling healthy, I started exercising every day and experienced a huge boost in confidence.... It's easy cooking, fun, healthy, and any teen could do it by themselves."

Quoted in Jane Brody, "Recipes to Set Teenagers on a Healthy Path," *New York Times,* December 14, 2009. www.nytimes.com/2009/12/15/health/15Brody.html?_r=1&scp=1&sq=sugar%20diet&st=cse.

artificial sweeteners can cause your body to store fat more readily. . . . Water doesn't contain caffeine, of course, but it is actually the best way to wake yourself up when fatigued, because when hydrated your body and mind are alert and awake. Cold water is especially helpful."[38]

Losing Weight

Teenagers and college students who apply what they have learned about nutrition to their own diets often find their health improves as a result of losing weight. This is because, although obesity increases a person's risk of heart disease, stroke, diabetes, and cancer, the increase in risk is not necessarily permanent. Overweight people of any age who lose weight can experience health benefits, including lower cholesterol levels, lower blood sugar levels, and lower blood pressure—as well as more energy. Fifteen-year-old Dylan Baker of St. Louis, Missouri, did just that. He attended a weight management program at St. Louis Children's Hospital called Head to Toe. There he learned what constitutes a balanced diet and how to adjust his diet to help him manage his weight and improve his overall health.

Following the advice of the dieticians at the Head to Toe program, Dylan made changes to his diet. The changes he made were modest, but they were enough to turn his health around. He still eats hamburgers, but he makes sure to include fruits and vegetables in his meals, too. He also keeps his portion sizes of meats, fats, and sugars at moderate levels.

"If I'm going to have a burger for lunch," Dylan says now, "I'm going to have something healthier to eat for dinner, like a salad."[39] When he eats meat, Dylan tries to make sure that he has a piece that is no bigger than a deck of cards.

No matter how determined overweight teenagers are to lose weight, they often need the help of their families in order for the weight-loss effort to be successful. Dylan's family began shopping together, helping each other to choose healthy foods and keeping track of the number of calories in the grocery cart. With his family to help him, Dylan lost 15 pounds (6.8kg) in six months. His cholesterol levels went down, too. With all his extra energy, Dylan tried out for the school baseball team and made it. "If it wasn't for what I did to get healthy, I probably wouldn't have tried out for the school team,"[40] he says. Now Dylan plays in the outfield.

Recovery from Depression

Sometimes people's dietary choices can affect their mental well-being as well as their physical health. Like many young teenage girls, British celebrity Shazzie decided in high school that she wanted to become a vegetarian. She wound up discovering the hard way that simply avoiding meat does not guarantee a person good health. Shazzie was a vegetarian who did not eat vegetables—and she did not feel very healthy. "When I was 16, I became a vegetarian," Shazzie wrote later. "As I stopped eating meat I started eating cheese, cheese and more cheese (as well as crackers and pasta)."[41] After several years on her cheese and pasta diet, Shazzie had gained quite a bit of weight and had developed a bad case of acne. She was tired all the time, caught between four and six cold or flu viruses per year, had a short attention span, and felt as though her energy was always very low. Her blood pressure started to go up.

Worst of all, Shazzie was struggling with major depression. "Sometimes I don't know how I got through the day, sometimes I didn't get through the day," she says. "I would come home at night and cry and cry and cry."[42]

Eating plenty of fruits and vegetables can often help a person deal with the depression that comes from being overweight.

One day Shazzie happened to find a book on nutrition. Flipping through the book, she realized that she was deficient in almost every vitamin or mineral mentioned. She started eating more fruits, along with lots of salad. At the same time, she did more research on nutrition. Gradually, Shazzie became convinced that what she really needed was to eat a diet based around raw fruits and vegetables. The change turned her life around. She lost weight and her acne disappeared. Then the depression disappeared, too. She calls it a fantastic feeling. "I remember feeling depressed, but that enormous black cloud which used to engulf me had long gone from my memory," she recalls. "It took me a while to recover, and it still seems like a dream that I don't have to sleep in the middle of the day, and my aches and pains are barely there."[43] Like Shazzie, many teenagers and young adults have found they can recover from chronic health problems by changing their lifestyle and eating more fruits and vegetables.

Changing the World

Many teens, and even younger children, are not satisfied with only improving their own diets and health. They want to make a change for the better in the diets of others in the world, too. In Upton, Kentucky, an elementary school class decided that they would end their study of farm animals by raising money to send a farm animal to a poor family. They began raking leaves, sweeping sidewalks, and washing dishes to earn money. Ultimately, the class earned $120, enough to send a sheep to a family through Heifer International, an organization that specializes in sending donated farm animals to poor rural families around the world. In this way, the young students were able to help improve the diet of a family in rural Rwanda.

Older students are also working to help improve the diet of others. College students often have the chance to go in person to faraway locations and intern with organizations that are working to reduce poverty and malnutrition in developing countries. One student from Cornell University, interning with the United Nations World Food Programme in Rome, developed his own vulnerability index—a way to assess how much danger of famine and poverty different countries were in as a result of the worsening world economic crisis.

Students who volunteer with the Peace Corps, as well, may have the chance to make a difference in the diet of a community. Peace Corps volunteers often work with farmers to encourage them to plant crops that are rich in micronutrients such as vitamin A, iron, or iodine. Dana Carson helped subsistence farmers in Nicaragua to plant trees and grasses on hillsides to prevent soil erosion. "These efforts have helped to stabilize their traditional crops," she writes. "In addition, we are introducing new produce such as tomato, onion, and cabbage."[44]

Michael Tidwell, who volunteered with the Peace Corps in Zaire, helped the chief of a village to dig a fish pond to provide food for his community. Tidwell writes: "When the last of the 300 tilapia fingerlings had entered the new pond, I turned to Ilunga and shook his hand over and over again. We ran around the banks hooting and hollering, laughing like children, watching the fish and marveling at what a wonderful thing a pond was."[45]

Students at the University of Michigan have the chance to intern with another international organization, the William Davidson Institute Global Impact program. In June 2009 intern Patrick Fay blogged about his experience working with the program in Lima, Peru. Fay worked with an entrepreneur to build a business selling dried anchovies and helping him to analyze whether the business was likely to make a profit. Fay not only considered how the entrepreneur's business would generate profits but also how it would provide needed nutrients

NUTRITION FACT

Less than $22,050

The official definition of "poor" in the United States means that a family of four people has less than $22,050 to live on for the year. About 19 percent, or 14 million, live in families that are classified as poor.

Teen Health News Show

Teenagers at Roosevelt Senior High School in Washington, D.C., decided to start their own audiovisual news show to raise awareness about good nutrition and healthy lifestyle choices. Students were proud of their creation, which was entirely conceived and written by Roosevelt High communications students. Students divided the show into four fifteen-minute programs that were each split up into four segments. The segments provided short factoids about healthy lifestyles, which helped the students make informed choices when it came to eating and exercise.

Show producer Sharon Quick wondered how students would come up with funding to pay for producing the show, but several organizations contacted them to offer support when they heard about it. "When they found out inner city youth were doing video, people called us," Quick remarked later. "They were looking for that other voice." The Metropolitan Police Department, Women in Film and Video Image Makers, D.C. Campaign to Prevent Teen Pregnancy, and My Sister's Place all offered to help support the students' efforts.

Quoted in Azure Thompson, "Teens Take Control of Their Media Image Through Innovative Health Show," *Washington Afro-American*, November 17, 2000. www.encyclopedia.com/doc/1P1-79666570.html.

Roosevelt High School offers culinary classes where students learn how to cook healthy meals.

for the community. He looked at the protein and healthy fat content of the food and wrote:

> Pablo plans to sell 1 Kg of dried anchovies for 1 nuevo sol (=33 cents), with a 30% profit margin. His business model is very interesting and seems to make a lot of sense in this market because it satisfies an unmet need for protein sources suitable to people with few economic resources. Many of the potential clients work as farmers or fishermen and do not have refrigerators for storing meat. The advantages of dried anchovies are that they have incredibly high nutritional value (protein, omega 3, omega 6, vitamin C), cost little (raw cost of anchovies in Caral is about 10 cents per pound), and can last for months without going rotten once they have been dried.[46]

When young adults return from internships in developing countries, they sometimes are frustrated to find that their views on nutrition and development are not taken seriously by established business groups at home. "We need to step away from the cliché that youth should be placed in the kiddy corner," one former intern writes, "while world leaders make decisions on our futures."[47] Some agencies and corporations, though, are beginning to involve young people when it comes to making decisions about nutrition and health. "The World Bank and all the other different organizations like the [United Nations], the FAO, have been increasing their emphasis on involving young people," writes Saadia Iqbal, who edits the Youthink! website for the World Bank, an international organization that gives loans and advice to developing countries. International organizations, says Iqbal, are "not just investing money in youth or seeing them as an issue to solve but really engaging them and getting their ideas."[48]

To get ideas from young people, the Global Humanitarian Forum has opened up a website that has a youth forum in order to encourage young people to present their ideas for changing the world. The forum has worked to get young people admitted to high-level meetings and conferences,

where they can meet policy makers from around the world and present their ideas on improving nutrition and diet around the world. "We want to give young people a chance to interact directly with . . . high level personalities," says the Youth Forum's project manager, Mischa Liatowitsch, "so young people can learn from the older generation and vice versa."[49]

As young people learn more about nutrition, they at first tend to feel empowered by the prospect of being able to reverse the progress of some diseases or at least manage them through good nutrition. A person's body may seem as though it has suddenly acquired a magical ability to heal itself. Preventing disease or healing from malnutrition is not

Teenagers can become empowered from managing good nutrition and a healthy lifestyle.

magic, however, and teenagers do not have to be magicians to make those kinds of transformations occur. All they have to do is eat a rainbow of fresh fruits and vegetables every day, along with whole grains, healthy fats, and healthy sources of protein. Upon realizing this, most young people quickly recognize the need to find ways to provide good quality food for struggling and impoverished communities around the world—and they are eager to put their minds, and their hands, to that task.

Introduction: Diet's Impact on Disease

1. Joseph Alpert, "Failing Grades in the Adoption of Healthy Lifestyle Choices," *American Journal of Medicine*, June 2009. www.amjmed.com/ article/S0002-9343(09)00093-X/ fulltext.
2. Jeffrey McCombs, "A 'S.A.D.' Lifestyle," *Huffington Post,* November 17, 2008. www.huffingtonpost .com/dr-jeffrey-mccombs/a-sad-life style_b_144395.html.
3. William Sears, "Standard American Diet (SAD)," AskDr.Sears. www.ask drsears.com/html/4/t044900.asp.

Chapter 1: Four Diseases Diet Could Prevent

4. Quoted in Bill Geist, "A Meal to Die For," CBS News, December 29, 2008. www.cbsnews.com/video/ watch/?id=4632991n?source=most pop_video.
5. Geist, "A Meal to Die For."
6. Quoted in Geist, "A Meal to Die For."
7. Quoted in *ScienceDaily*, "Obesity and Diabetes Double Risk of Heart Failure: Patients with Both Conditions 'Very Difficult' to Treat," June 4, 2009. www.sciencedaily.com/ releases/2009/05/090530094510 .htm.
8. Desiree Dizadji, interview by author, February 10, 2010.
9. Quoted in Amanda Gardner, "Obesity Rolling Back Gains in Heart Health," MedicineNet, November 17, 2009. www.medicinenet.com/script/ main/art.asp?articlekey=107735.
10. Quoted in *ScienceDaily*, "Obesity and Diabetes Double Risk of Heart Failure."
11. Quoted in Useful Information, "Quotations About Food." www .useful-information.info/quotations/ food_quotes.html.

Chapter 2: Diet and Deficiencies

12. Quoted in Paul Virgo, "Development: Hunger Feeds More Hunger," Inter Press Service News Agency, January 22, 2010. www.ipsnews.net/ news.asp?idnews=50071.
13. Quoted in Denise Mann, "Vitamin D Deficiency Common in U.S. Children," CNNHealth, August 3, 2009. www.cnn.com/2009/ HEALTH/08/03/vitamin.d.children.

Chapter 3: How Diet Can Prevent Disease

14. Quoted in *ScienceDaily*, "Longer Life Linked to Specific Foods in Mediterranean Diet," June 24, 2009. www.sciencedaily.com/releases/2009/06/090624093353.htm.

15. Quoted in *ScienceDaily*, "Longer Life Linked to Specific Foods in Mediterranean Diet."

16. Quoted in Dan Childs, "Take It or Leave It? The Truth About 8 Mediterranean Diet Staples," ABC News, June 24, 2009. http://abcnews.go.com/Health/MensHealthNews/story?id=7911505.

17. Quoted in *ScienceDaily*, "New Evidence of How High Glucose Damages Blood Vessels Could Lead to New Treatments," May 12, 2009. www.sciencedaily.com/releases/2009/05/090511140951.htm.

18. National Heart, Lung, and Blood Institute, "Guide to Behavior Change." www.nhlbi.nih.gov/health/public/heart/obesity/lose_wt/behavior.htm.

19. Quoted in *Medical News*, "Obesity and Heart Failure Risk," May 1, 2008. www.news-medical.net/news/2008/05/01/37984.aspx.

20. Quoted in *ScienceDaily*, "Phytochemicals in Plant-Based Foods Could Help Battle Obesity, Disease," October 22, 2009. www.sciencedaily.com/releases/2009/10/091021144251.htm.

21. Quoted in Ann Wang, "Plant Antioxidants Also Fight Inflammation," *Johns Hopkins News-Letter*, October 23, 2008. http://media.www.jhunewsletter.com/media/storage/paper932/news/2008/10/23/Science/Plant.Antioxidants.Also.Fight.Inflammation-3503169.shtml.

22. Quoted in *Heart Advisor*, "Add More Color to Your Diet: At the End of This Rainbow, Plates of Heart-Healthy Foods," HighBeam Research, February 1, 2006. www.highbeam.com/doc/1G1-144106222.html.

23. Quoted in Bev Bennett, "The Green Defense," HighBeam Research, November 8, 2000. www.highbeam.com/doc/1P2-4561974.html.

Chapter 4: What Governments and Organizations Are Doing

24. Quoted in WebMD, "Metabolic Syndrome Common in Obese Children," CBS News, June 25, 2008. www.cbsnews.com/stories/2008/06/26/health/webmd/main4212423.shtml.

25. Alpert, "Failing Grades in the Adoption of Healthy Lifestyle Choices."

26. Quoted in PR Newswire, "New Definition Helps Identify Children at Risk of Metabolic Syndrome," June 25, 2007. www.prnewswire.com/news-releases/new-definition-helps-identify-children-at-risk-of-metabolic-syndrome-59351112.html.

27. Quoted in Fran Lowry, "Beta-Cell Abnormalities Predict Type 2 Diabetes in Obese Teens," *Internal

Medicine News, November 1, 2008, p. 18.

28. Quoted in Elizabeth Heubeck, "Fatty Liver Disease Escalates in Children," *DOC News*, September 2007. http://docnews.diabetesjournals .org/content/4/9/9.full.

29. Quoted in Paul Swiech, "Making Smart Choices: The Smart Choices Checkmark Will Begin Appearing on the Front of Food Packages This Month, an Effort by a Broad-Based Coalition to Help Americans Choose Healthier Foods," AllBusiness, August 11, 2009. www .allbusiness.com/medicine-health/ diet-nutrition-fitness/12637243-1 .html.

30. Quoted in *New York Daily News*, "Obese Children Have Arteries of 45-Year-Olds, Study Finds," November 12, 2008. www.nydaily news.com/lifestyle/health/ 2008/11/12/2008-11-12_obese_ children_have_arteries_of_45year ol.html.

31. Quoted in Nanci Hellmich, "Health Movement Has School Cafeterias in a Food Fight," *USA Today*, August 21, 2005. www.usatoday .com/news/health/2005-08-21- junk-food-cover_x.htm.

32. Quoted in Mary MacVean, "Congress May Bolster School Lunch Nutrition," *Los Angeles Times*, August 26, 2009. http://articles .latimes.com/2009/aug/26/nation/ na-child-nutrition26.

33. Quoted in Kate MacArthur, "Fast-Food Goes on Health Kick; Chains Address Nutrition to Avoid Regulation," AllBusiness, April 28, 2003. www.allbusiness.com/medicine-health/health-health-care-by-target/9393187-1.html.

34. Quoted in Carole Sharwarko, "Fast-Food Giant to Post Nutrition Information," HighBeam Research, October 2, 2008. www.highbeam .com/doc/1N1-123EB4BFFA18 21A0.html.

Chapter 5: Teens Making a Difference Through Diet

35. Quoted in Jacqueline Adams, "A Heart Healthy Dinner Date: Want to Wow Your Valentine? Serve Up This Nutritious Meal from the Nation's Best Teen Chef," HighBeam Research, February 4, 2008. www.highbeam.com/ doc/1G1-174061880.html.

36. Jane Brody, "Recipes to Set Teenagers on a Healthy Path," *New York Times*, December 14, 2009. www.nytimes .com/2009/12/15/health/15Brody .html?_r=1&scp=1&sq=sugar%20 diet&st=cse.

37. Quoted in Reuters, "Potassium Can 'Normalize' Teen Blood Pressure," Reuters Health eLine, May 20, 1998.

38. Quoted in Kathryn Gregory, "Students Find Healthier Alternatives to Soda," HighBeam Research, April 4, 2006. www.highbeam.com/ doc/1P1-121295117.html.

39. Quoted in Stephen Smith, "Pound for Pound: When This Teen Learned He Was Overweight, He Embraced

the Challenge of Living a Healthy Lifestyle," HighBeam Research, February 1, 2009. www.encyclopedia.com/doc/1G1-192850419.html.

40. Quoted in Smith, "Pound for Pound."

41. Shazzie, "Why I Went Raw in 2000," Shazzie.com, January 2009. www.shazzie.com/life/articles/why_raw.shtml.

42. Shazzie, "Why I Went Raw in 2000."

43. Shazzie, "Why I Went Raw in 2000."

44. Quoted in Peace Corps, "Profile: Dana Carson and Ed Chew," September 29, 2008. www.peacecorps.gov/index.cfm?shell=learn.whatlike.story&story_id=359&assign_cat_id=4&dis_code=0.

45. Michael Tidwell, "The Joy of Digging," Peace Corps, September 29, 2008. www.peacecorps.gov/index.cfm?shell=learn.whatlike.story&story_id=1225&assign_cat_id=4&dis_code=0.

46. Patrick Fay, "Caral Caral Caral," WDI Global Impact Internship Program, June 30, 2009. http://mblog.lib.umich.edu/WDIGlobalImpact/archives/2009/06/index.html.

47. Quoted in Andrew Baxter, "Development: Organisations Wake Up to the Potential of Young Perspectives," *Financial Times*, January 28, 2010. www.ft.com/cms/s/0/0b1a45a0-0b63-11df-8232-00144feabdc0.html.

48. Quoted in Baxter, "Development."

49. Quoted in Baxter, "Development."

amino acids: The building blocks of proteins, used by the body to grow new tissue and to keep the brain and nervous system healthy.

antioxidant: A substance that can reduce inflammation in the body.

atherosclerosis: The buildup of fatty deposits and plaque in the arteries, which makes the arteries narrow and hard.

carbohydrates: Foods that provide energy, such as starches and sugars.

carcinogen: A substance that causes cancer.

cardiovascular: Related to the heart and blood vessels.

cholesterol: A type of fat that circulates in the blood.

junk food: Foods that are dense in calories but low in nutrients.

macrominerals: Minerals that the body needs in large amounts rather than trace amounts.

macronutrients: The basic raw materials that the body needs.

metabolic syndrome: A condition in which the body has multiple risk factors for both heart disease and type 2 diabetes, including at least three of the following risk factors: too much fat around the waist, high blood pressure, high blood sugar, high levels of fat in the blood, and abnormal cholesterol levels.

minerals: Elements such as calcium, iron, and magnesium.

obese: Usually defined as being more than 19 percent heavier than one's ideal body weight.

overweight: Being up to 19 percent heavier than one's ideal body weight.

The American Cancer Society

1599 Clifton Rd. NE
Atlanta, GA 30322
phone: (404) 327-5712
website: www.cancer.org

The American Cancer Society provides the public with information about cancer. Its website includes information about every major type of cancer, including causes, symptoms, diagnosis, and treatment. The American Cancer Society also advocates for and does fund-raising on behalf of cancer research.

American Diabetes Association

1701 N. Beauregard St.
Alexandria, VA 22311
phone: (800) 342-2383
website: www.diabetes.org

The American Diabetes Association provides information to patients, caregivers, families, health-care professionals, and researchers. It also advocates for and does fund-raising on behalf of research to treat and prevent diabetes.

American Dietetic Association

120 S. Riverside Plaza, Suite 2000
Chicago, IL 60606-6995
phone: (800) 877-1600
website: www.eatright.org

The American Dietetic Association is the world's largest association of nutritionists and dieticians. It provides information about nutrition to the public, students, the media, and health-care professionals.

American Heart Association

National Center

7272 Greenville Ave.
Dallas, TX 75231
phone: (800) 242-8721
website: www.americanheart.org

The American Heart Association provides information about cardiovascular disease to the public, patients, caregivers, health-care professionals, researchers, and scientists. It also advocates for and does fund-raising on behalf of research to treat and prevent heart disease.

American Public Health Association

800 I St. NW
Washington, DC 20001-3710
phone: (202) 777-2742
website: www.apha.org

The American Public Health Association is an organization that works to protect the health of Americans through programs that provide education and preventive health services to communities.

American Stroke Association

National Center
7272 Greenville Ave.
Dallas, TX 75231
phone: (888) 478-7653
website: www.strokeassociation.org

The American Stroke Association offers support and information to stroke patients, caregivers, families, and health-care professionals. It also advocates for and does fund-raising on behalf of research to treat and prevent strokes.

National Institutes of Health (NIH)

9000 Rockville Pike
Bethesda, MD 20892
phone: (301) 496-4000
website: www.nih.gov

The NIH is a major branch of the US Department of Health and Human Services. Its primary function is to conduct and support medical research. Its website provides a wide range of information, including detailed sections on topics targeting teen health. It also offers an RSS feed, e-mail updates, downloads, and more.

School Nutrition Association

700 S. Washington St., Suite 300
Alexandria, VA 22314-4287
phone: (703) 739-3900
website : www.schoolnutrition.org

The School Nutrition Association website contains news related to nutrition in schools, such as school lunch and breakfast programs, programs to combat childhood obesity, and legislation related to school nutrition.

FOR MORE INFORMATION

Books

Toney Allman, *Nutrition and Disease Prevention*. New York: Chelsea House, 2010. Explores the relationship between the way people eat and the development, as well as prevention, of disease.

Roberta Duyff, *American Dietetic Association Complete Food and Nutrition Guide*. New York: Wiley, 2006. Includes updated scientific advice about what foods are best for the body, guidelines for weight control, guidelines for eating healthfully in restaurants, and an explanation of how diet is connected to chronic diseases. Also explains how some foods and drugs interact and how food allergies work.

Carrie Fredericks, *Obesity*. San Diego, CA: ReferencePoint, 2008. Includes information on the health consequences, treatment, prevention, and causes of obesity. Also explains the degree to which lifestyle choices can influence body weight.

Patrick Holford, *Optimum Nutrition for the Mind*. Bergen, NJ: Basic Health, 2004. A review of research into how nutrition affects the brain, with special attention paid to amino acids and their relationship to neurotransmitters.

M.N. Jimerson, *Childhood Obesity*. Detroit: Lucent, 2008. Part of the Diseases and Disorders series, this book provides an overview of the causes and the health effects of childhood obesity.

Robert Ronzio, *The Encyclopedia of Nutrition and Good Health*. New York: Facts On File, 2005. A comprehensive encyclopedia of foods and food ingredients, written by a biochemist. Each entry explains how a particular ingredient is used by the body and what effects it has on the body, including the body's brain chemistry.

Walter C. Willett and P.J. Skerrett, *Eat, Drink, and Be Healthy: The Harvard Medical School Guide to Healthy Eating*. New York: Free Press, 2002. A book of recommendations for healthy eating based mainly on the results of large scientific studies. Willett provides his own healthy eating pyramid, which recommends that the foundation of the diet be vegetables and fruits.

Websites

American Cancer Society (www.can cer.org). Includes facts and statistics about all kinds of cancer, information about clinical trials, a guide to quitting smoking, information about healthy diet and lifestyle choices, links to fund-raisers intended to raise money for cancer research, and news about recent research related to cancer. Also includes specialized information for cancer patients and their families.

American Diabetes Association (www .diabetes.org). Explains the differences between type 1 and type 2 diabetes, how diabetes develops, and how to manage diabetes through diet and lifestyle changes. Also includes recipes and information about recent news and research.

American Heart Association (www .americanheart.org). Includes information about diseases and conditions that are caused by cardiovascular disease, as well as news about research being done on cardiovascular disease, advice concerning a healthy diet and lifestyle, and a section devoted to children's health. Also includes a social media application designed to encourage people to do more walking.

Centers for Disease Control and Prevention: "How Many Fruits & Vegetables Do You Need?" (www .fruitsandveggiesmatter.gov). Every person's body is different, so recommended daily fruit and vegetable intake varies from one person to another. The Centers for Disease Control and Prevention has put up an online RDA calculator to use in determining the right amount.

Let's Move! (www.letsmove.gov). The *Let's Move!* campaign, started by First Lady Michelle Obama, is a nationwide initiative to promote making healthy lifestyle choices; improving food quality in schools; increasing access to healthy, affordable food; and getting kids more physically active. The website provides nutrition information as well as fun ways for kids to get more exercise.

Nutrition Data (www.nutritiondata .com). Includes detailed nutrition information for commonly eaten foods, including nutrition information for entrées on many restaurant menus. Nutrition information provided for food includes an analysis of how each nutrient compares with the recommended daily allowances; a breakdown of what percentage of the food's calories come from carbohydrates, fats, and protein; the estimated glycemic load (a measure of how a food affects blood sugar levels); and a numeric measurement of how full the food is likely to make a person feel.

Nutrition.gov (www.nutrition.gov). The federal government's website on nutrition. Includes information provided by the USDA, the Department of Health and Human Services, and other government agencies. It contains links to information about the food guide pyramid, the dietary guidelines for Americans, and information about the safety of vitamin and mineral supplements.

PICTURE CREDITS

ABOUT THE AUTHOR

Bonnie Juettner is a writer and editor with a strong interest in science and health. She regularly writes for Lucent's Diseases and Disorders series, writes a health column for Examiner.com, and is a frequent contributor to websites focused on nutritional approaches to good health.